# Crystal Skull
## *Message Card Meditations*

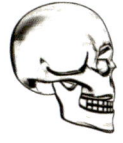 

Created by
White Elk Woman
&
Lorenzo Guescini

Published by Mystic Mouse® Publishing in 2014
www.MysticMouse-Publishing.com

Text Copyright © 2014 White Elk Woman & L.Guescini

Image Copyright © 2007 -14 White Elk Woman & L.Guescini

First Edition

The author asserts the moral right under the Copyright, Designs and Patents Act 1988 to be identified as the author of this work.

All rights reserved. No part of this publication may be reproduced, stored in a retrieval system or transmitted, in any form or by any means without the prior consent of the author, nor be otherwise circulated in any form of binding or cover other than that which it is published and without a similar condition being imposed on the subsequent purchaser.

Mystic Mouse® is a registered trademark of Mystic Mouse® Ltd

> The author and publisher accept no responsibility for how you might use the images or information contained herein or any results that may occur.
>
> It is the intention of the author to offer only general help & guidance towards your physical, mental, spiritual and emotional growth and wellbeing.

# Image Index

|  | Page |  | Page |
|---|---|---|---|
| Abundance Island | 25 | Obelisk | 67 |
| Air | 27 | Om | 69 |
| Ancestors | 29 | Pi | 71 |
| Ascension Earth | 31 | Protection | 73 |
| Blue Skull | 33 | Rainbow | 75 |
| Communication | 35 | Recycle | 77 |
| DNA | 37 | Sacred Space | 79 |
| Download | 39 | Star | 81 |
| Earth | 41 | Teleportation | 83 |
| 11:11 Rebirth | 43 | The Mirror | 85 |
| 11:11 Transformation | 45 | The Observatory | 87 |
| Fire | 47 | The Temple | 89 |
| Guiding Lights | 49 | The Void | 91 |
| Imagination | 51 | Thirteen Skulls | 93 |
| Individuality | 53 | Time | 95 |
| Labyrinth | 55 | Tree of Knowledge | 97 |
| Lotus Flower | 57 | Trusted Friend | 99 |
| Magenta Bridge | 59 | Two Worlds | 101 |
| Moon Phases | 61 | Violet Flame | 103 |
| Nature | 63 | Voyage of Discovery | 105 |
| Perception | 65 | Water | 107 |

## An Introduction to the Crystal Skulls

Crystal Skulls have been around for thousands of years. Many believe the Ancient Skulls (which cannot be dated) were created by 'light beings', through a process of thought and intent, or perhaps by beings from another time or planet with far superior technology. Books on the subject, as well as skull caretakers themselves, often make reference to the fact that there is something 'other worldly' about the skulls and it seems likely that there is a connection between skulls, crop circles, ceremonial stone sites and the stars.

One thing we know for sure is that there is so much more to learn from crystal skulls of the past, present & future, both spiritually & practically.

## A note from White Elk Woman…

Why Crystal Skull Message Card Meditations? If you have ever found yourself saying any of the following, I think you will understand why we created this book.

> - There are times when I feel so different and alone.
> - It seems as if people don't really understand me.
> - I have so many great ideas… but I just can't seem to bring them into reality.
> - I don't feel like I know who am I, or what I am supposed to be doing.
> - I know there are things I need to share with the world, but I don't know how.

I've had all of these thoughts on my journey with the Crystal Skulls, some many times, and it has been a constant 'evolution'. The path I chose was sometimes challenging, but it was always full of learning, transformation and growth.

Having been a Medium, Soul Healer, Spiritual Counsellor, Shaman, Workshop Leader and Event Organiser, I officially took on a new role as a Crystal Skull Caretaker in 2004.

My spiritual evolution continued on the 'fast track' and, in 2008 when the original **Crystal Skull Message Cards** were born, I added Lightworker, Wayshower, Author and Company Director to the list. In 2010, the Crystal Skull **Shadow*Light* Cards** and **Personal & Planetary Healing with Crystal Skulls CD** were released and I was able to tap into my life long passion for music and sound.

The point I'm making is that it is okay to be different, it's okay to have tried, been or done many things, but sometimes being on the crest of that particular wave can seem lonely.

My journey has taken many paths, and more recently my choices have included professional public speaking and charity fundraising. Curiously, I had not been working with Crystal Skulls consciously for over two years until, on Easter Sunday 2014, I awoke with what felt like a directive from Andromeda, one of my crystal starbeings. She showed me a new path and I had a choice to make...

I chose to create this book for you and, honestly, if I can choose to set up a successful self-publishing company with no idea where to start and a huge dislike (at the time) for anything that involved business, writing or paperwork, I know that you can choose to make your dreams and visions happen too!

You have choices… and whatever you experience is up to you. You have the power to change, in any given moment.

So, how will you choose to feel today?

And what will you choose to do?

*White Elk Woman*

# Two FREE gifts especially for you!
## from White Elk Woman

Come visit me on **The Entrepreneurial Lightworker** website where you will find two FREE videos that I've created especially for you!

**Working with the Crystal Skull Shadow*Light* Cards**
This video gives you in depth guidance on how to easily and effortlessly clear underlying and unresolved issues or emotions - Turning your 'Shadows' into '*Light*'.

**How to get the most from the
Crystal Skull Message Card Meditations**
This video gives you guidance on how to work in greater depth with this book and the Crystal Skull Collective. It will help you to get the most out of each image, along with a deeper understanding of the colour bars, the numerology, and affirmations.

www.TheEntrepreneurialLightworker.com

See you there!
Many Blessings

Continue your journey with the Crystal Skulls by connecting with some of our friends from around the world, who live and work with Crystal Skulls, sharing their knowledge, love and wisdom:

**Millennium** - Maurice Dunner
Your source for highest quality Crystal Skulls - USA/ Canada
**www.crystalskulls.com**

**Divining Me -** Shirley Sienna Coventry
Illumination & Enlightenment through the Crystal Skulls - Melbourne, Australia
**www.shirleysienna.com**

**Kristallikallot -** Anna-Maija & Juha Laukkanen
Retailers of Crystal Bowls & Crystal Skulls - Finland
**www.shamballa.fi**

**Krystal's -** Joe & Marylee Swanson
Crystal Skull retailers for over 25 years - Colorado USA
**joekrystals1982@gmail.com**

**Bodhiella Creations -** Elizabeth Gardiepy
Crystal Skull meditations, healing & readings - Oregon USA
**www.bodhiella.com**

**2 Blue's - 'Dare 2B Crystal'**
**'Guardeepers'** for a loving Crystal Head Family
*Blue Arrow Rainbow White Eagle Feather:*
**CrystalHeads4LOVE@xs4all.nl**
*Blue EagleWolf:*
**BlueCosmicAmethyst-CrystalHead@hotmail.com**

## Before working with this book

You may wish to hold the book to your heart when you first receive it and bond with it in a positive and loving way, holding the intention that the pages within will always work with you for the highest good of all concerned.

If you are going to be using these images when working with other people, either for healing or interpretation and guidance, then you might like to sit with an image each day and really get to know the healing energy and information that it brings through. Although each image already has some channelled guidance, you may well find that each sitting brings something very different. So just go with the flow and learn to trust that what is given is exactly as it should be.

Before choosing an image to work with, sit quietly, relax and take a few deep breaths. Ask to be connected to the Crystal Skull Collective in order that they work with and through you in the best way possible at this time.

Hold a clear intention of what it is you would like to receive guidance or healing on during a session. Then, when you feel ready, just start to flick through the book and see where you 'land'. You may be drawn to the image in the top right hand corner or the coloured tabs at the edge of the page, or the book may just fall open at a particular place. You may even hear or see a page number in your head.

There is no right or wrong way to use this book, just go with what you feel is right and true in your heart and let the Crystal Skull Collective do the rest…

# Using this book

The following pages provide some basic information to get you started, but the more you work with these images, the more you will understand their vibrations. Each image is accompanied by a message of support, love & guidance from the skull(s) pictured, along with questions to meditate on. The colour vibrations can also be used to bring about healing on many levels.

Working with these images, you could...

- Focus on the image and allow yourself to be drawn in. Feel its energy wash over and through you.
- Place the image within your aura as you feel guided.
- If working with a client, breathe in the colour(s) and blow the vibrations into their aura.

For more guidance on how to work with this book, take a look at our online videos - see page 10 for details.

# Affirmations

Each image comes with two Affirmations you might like to try. It is usually a good idea to say these daily (either out loud or in your mind) for 30 days, or at least until you really start to feel that a particular affirmation has been integrated into your actual experience. You can also breathe in the colour in the Affirmations box to enhance the words as you say them.

## Chakras and Colours

This section provides some basic guidelines as to how the colour vibrations relate to the chakras and consequently various parts of your body (as well as states of mind, spirit or emotion). By integrating the various colour vibrations in the images, you can help to bring harmony to these areas.

As a chakra could be overactive or underactive or even in trauma, you may sometimes wish to consider working with the opposite (complementary) colour as this may help calm an overactive or traumatised energy centre. The colour tabs on the edge of each page provide an example of an energising colour (lower tab) and calming colour (upper tab). As always, there is no absolute right or wrong way to work with these, so just allow yourself to be a clear channel, trust, and let the images and colours speak to you.

A list of the seven main chakras and their approximate positions is included in this section. You can also find examples of the things that might be experienced if a chakra is out of balance and how bringing appropriate colours into the related chakra can potentially enhance certain traits or emotions and aid certain physical issues.

### 1. Base

Some signs of imbalance may be: instability, insecurity, hunger/weight gain, lower back/leg/knee/spine problems, constipation, inability to manifest or move forward.

**Energising Colours:** Red, brown and earthy colours - can instil grounding, stability, stamina, motivation, purpose, strength, manifestation.

## 2. Sacral

Some signs of imbalance may be: jealousy, frustration, sexual problems and allergies. Skin, bladder and lower intestines may also be affected.

**Energising Colours:** Orange & autumnal colours - can instil joy, respect for oneself, creativity, cheer, pick-me-up, happiness. Can help to release stored negativity.

## 3. Solar Plexus

Some signs of imbalance may be: fear, lack of confidence, perfectionism, low self esteem, diabetes, ulcers. Digestion, nerves, liver and muscles can also be affected.

**Energising Colours:** Yellow and golden colours - can instil happiness, cheer, focus, will(power), enthusiasm, energy, self worth, mental clarity.

## 4. Heart

Some signs of imbalance may be: emotionally unstable, overly critical, inability to show or receive affection. Heart, arms, hands, blood and circulation can also be affected.

**Energising Colours:** Green & pink - can instil love and trust in yourself & others, harmony, peace, abundance, new beginnings. Can help to release heart related emotions.

### 5. Throat

Some signs of imbalance may be: communication issues, little discernment, ignorance. Thyroid, ear, neck, shoulder, lung, and throat can also be affected.

**Energising Colours:** Blue & turquoise - can instil a release of physical tension, better communication, peace, healing, honesty, calming, cleansing.

### 6. Third Eye (Brow)

Some signs of imbalance may be: cynicism, fear, lack of concentration, feeling detached, headaches, eye/nose problems (especially left eye), vivid or unpleasant dreams.

**Energising Colours:** Indigo & purple - can instil a sense of responsibility, spiritual transformation & understanding; also powerful vision, clairvoyance, wisdom.

### 7. Crown

Some signs of imbalance may be: depression, lack of enthusiasm/ inspiration, migraines, problem with right eye, confusion, forgetful, psychological imbalance.

**Energising Colours:** White or magenta & ultra violet - can instil clarity, cleansing and purity. Connection to Source / Divine guidance & universal energy.

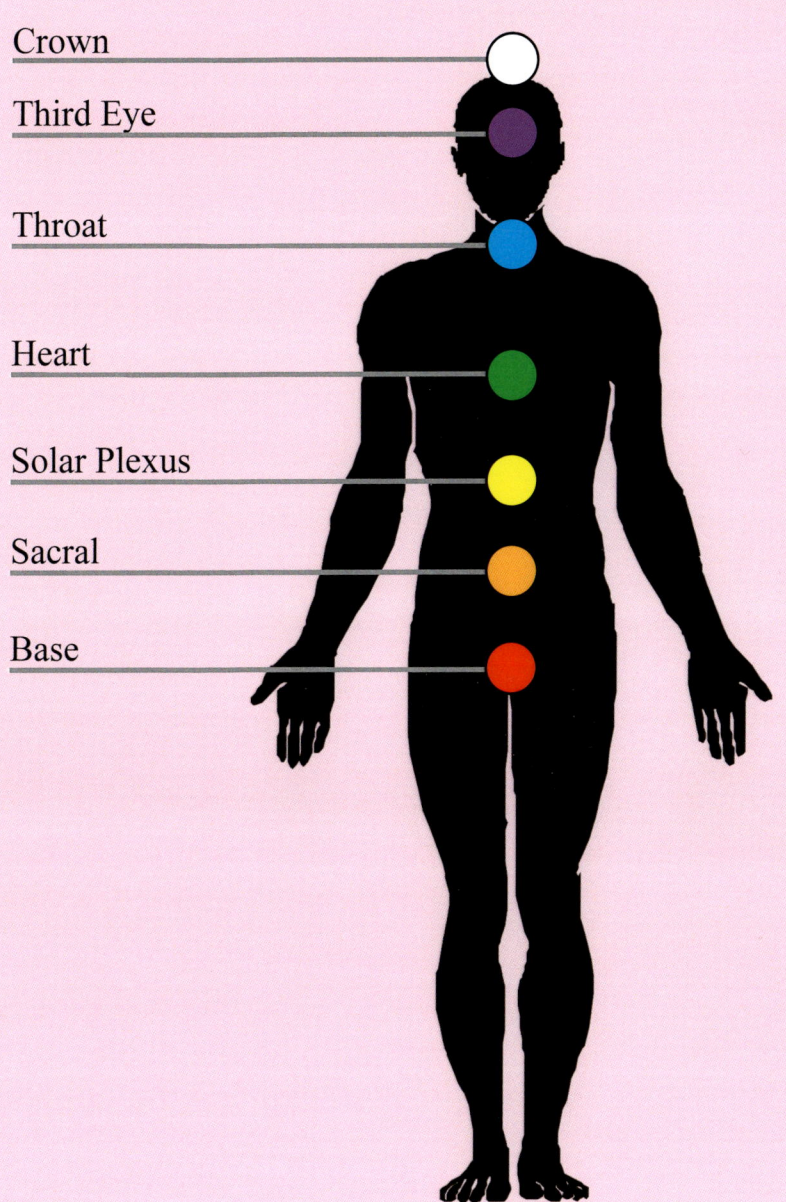

## The Aura

The body is not just physical, but is made up of various 'energetic' layers that can't be 'seen'. These layers make up the aura (also known as the auric field) and are called subtle energy bodies. Each layer relates to different aspects of the self. There are many subtle bodies, but most healers will perceive or work with the four main bodies (listed below).

○ 1. **The etheric body** sits within and directly around our physical body. This can be up to about an inch away and is usually the first part of the aura that people will see - often as a white, fuzzy glow around someone. It introduces energy to the physical and we can perceive the health and vitality of a person in this body.

● 2. **The emotional body** is where we hold most of our emotions, dreams and illusions. It is generally a few inches away from the physical. When linked in and giving healing, it can often be perceived either visually or simply as an intuitive sense of where it is.

○ 3. **The mental body** is slightly further out again and can be perceived in the same way. It is where our conscious and sub-conscious thoughts are held, both past and present. A finer vibration than the emotional, it can be perceived as bright yellow if it is healthy.

● 4. **The spiritual body** generally holds most of the wisdom and knowledge. This layer helps us acknowledge and bring in our guidance, angels and higher self etc. It is perceived as very pale hues of colour.

The etheric body feeds vitality to the physical body, while the emotional body can help bring creativity. The mental body can assist with structured thinking and the spiritual body is associated with wisdom. The emotional and mental bodies are quite strongly linked and it is often within one of these bodies that dis-ease starts. The aura can get very 'clogged & dirty'. This can come about through encountering negative people, places or thoughts. Working with particular images and colours can help to clear and balance the energy bodies within the aura, thus leading to an overall sense of vitality and wellbeing on all levels.

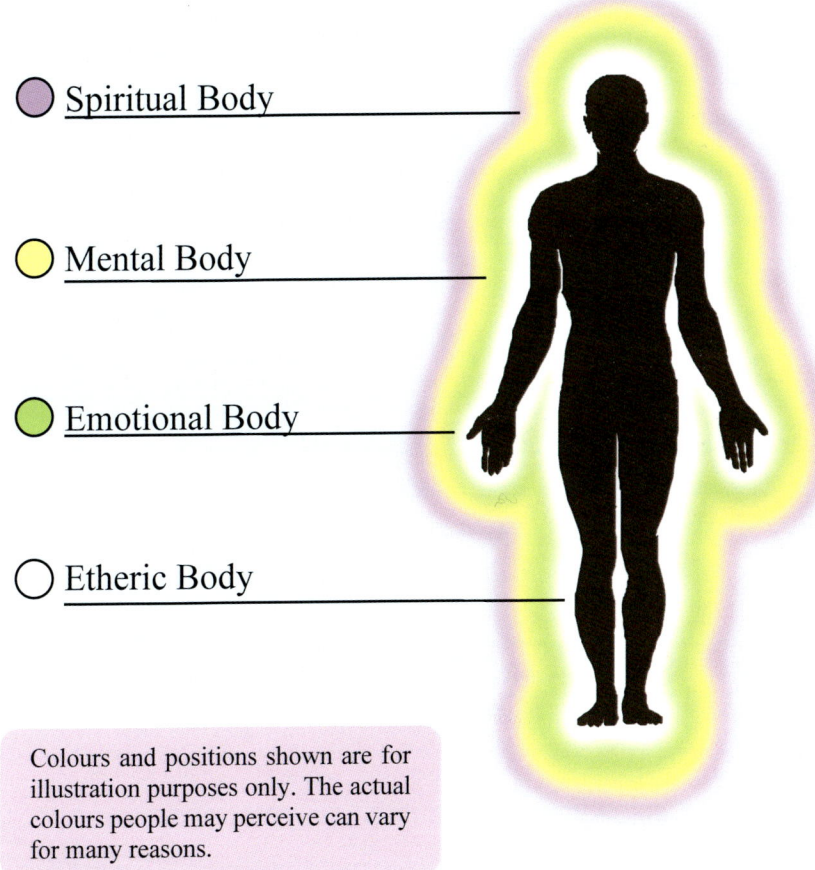

○ Spiritual Body

○ Mental Body

○ Emotional Body

○ Etheric Body

Colours and positions shown are for illustration purposes only. The actual colours people may perceive can vary for many reasons.

## Meditating to Resolve Issues

Sometimes just the act of meditating can seem to dissolve a problem. It can create a great space for dealing with issues in our lives and accessing our deep well of inner resources. However, if you find you have a more persistent issue, here are a couple of practical steps you can take:

1. Define the problem
2. Focus on the solution

### Defining the problem

Have you ever been in a situation where a friend has come to you with a problem and you can see the solution straight away? It seems so obvious that you wonder why they can't see it.

The issue here is that they have become stuck IN the problem. When you are stuck IN a problem, all you can see is the problem. You can't see the solution because the solution is always 'outside' of the problem. When you clearly define the problem, you create a boundary around it, making it easier to step outside of it.

Poorly defined problems can often be too vague to tackle effectively e.g. "I never seem to have enough money". When you use words like 'never' or 'always' it also seems to make the problem much bigger. By getting very specific, problems tend to shrink to a more manageable size e.g. "I need to deal with two unexpected bills this month".

## Focus on the solution

Once you are able to step outside of the problem by getting it clearly defined, you can start to tap into your inner resources to find the best solution.

Try meditating on the questions provided in this book to help gain clarity on specific issues - or create your own questions. When you formulate a question make sure you are focusing on the outcome you want, not the problem. It also helps to phrase the question so that it presupposes that the solution already exists. Example:

**Weak Question:** How can I solve this problem?

**Better Question:** What are the three fastest ways to achieve my desired outcome?

Relax and breathe deep as you go within and ask your question(s). Keep a pen and paper handy so that you can record any reactions, responses or insights.

You will find that some of the questions in this book are fairly direct, whilst others are purposefully vague or ambiguous. These questions give your mind permission to stretch out and get creative. Feel free to interpret the questions in any way you like. Don't get hung up on searching for 'the right answer', instead you are looking to expand your possibilities and illuminate new pathways.

# Your journey starts here...

# 1
## ঌ Abundance Island ཞ

*"Work with me to energise the heart, sacral & solar plexus and to help instil a sense of balance, harmony & passion"*

What does abundance look and feel like?

What resources are available to me right now to help me achieve abundance?

What are the things I appreciate most about myself?

---

### Affirmations

"I see with 'new eyes' all that surrounds me and I know that it is filled with love & beauty."

"Happiness, harmony & abundance abound in my life and I am truly grateful for all things, people & situations."

# 2
## ～ Air ～

*"Work with me for higher communication and to assist in bringing a sense of peace, serenity & inner tranquillity"*

What can I learn from Grandfather Sky and the bird kingdom today?

How could I change my perspective?

By gaining a new, clear perspective, what great visions come into view?

---

### Affirmations

"I relax my body, mind & emotions so I can reach the highest heights of my Spiritual Self."

"As I transcend, I ride the waves of love, lightness, inspiration & healing."

# 3
## ~ Ancestors ~

*"Work with us to bring energy & stability into the lower chakras and instil a sense of belonging & security"*

How best can I reconnect with my family, both past and present?

Where are my deepest connections at this time?

What gifts await me in the Aboriginal world of the dreamtime, or the worlds of the Shaman?

### Affirmations

"I have uncovered my roots and freely access the truth, wisdom & teachings from lifetimes past."

"I honour a change in my perception as to who true family are."

# 4
## ～ Ascension Earth ～

*"Work with me on the spiritual and mental bodies to instil a sense of stability, comfort & security"*

Am I currently ascending or descending on my path?

What important decisions will I make?

How do I experience my connection with the universe?

### Affirmations

"As I joyfully embrace this important spiritual transformation, I remain grounded whilst focusing on my broadening horizons."

"I see life and the universe from a new, unbiased perspective and feel deep appreciation for the healing work that is happening on Mother Earth."

# 5
## ⁙ Blue Skull ⁙

*"Work with me to energise the throat and heart chakras. I can help you understand your truth & path and feel comfortable sharing your messages with the world"*

How am I fulfilling my role as a guardian of the Earth?

What is the meaning of 'Oneness' to me?

How can I best speak my truth, walk my path and spread my light?

---

### Affirmations

"I follow the way of love, light, ascension and conscious evolution as I communicate with healing."

"I truly appreciate and understand what it means to live on, in and with this… my amazing Blue Planet."

# 6
## ᭥ Communication ᭣

*"Work with me to instil clarity and activate or energise the soul star, crown, third eye & throat chakras"*

When is meditation near the ocean beneficial for me?

How am I accessing the wisdom of Atlantis and Lemuria?

What soul messages do the whales and dolphins have for me?

### Affirmations

"I breathe deep and allow myself to experience inner peace and unconditional love."

"I listen intently to the sonic vibrations of the whales as they relay their soul messages and healing to me."

# 7
## ⌘ DNA ⌘

*"Work with us to activate and energise all chakras for an overall sense of wellbeing"*

What limiting beliefs and ancestral patterns have held me back in the past? And what new beliefs do I choose now?

What incredible untapped potential lies within me?

How can I unlock that great potential now?

## Affirmations

"I am now enjoying a happy and rewarding life, full of vitality."

"I activate my dormant DNA, unlocking my full potential."

# 8
## ~ Download ~

*"Work with us to energise the soul star, crown, third eye, throat & thymus for Divine Intervention, healing & wisdom on many levels"*

What new information is flowing to me right now?

How will I know that I am being downloaded?

Which skulls are currently connecting with each other and why?

---

### Affirmations

"I relax as the Crystal Skull Collective brings me what I need to know for my future learning."

"Every cell in my body is rejuvenating, regenerating and healing. I feel energised and totally alive."

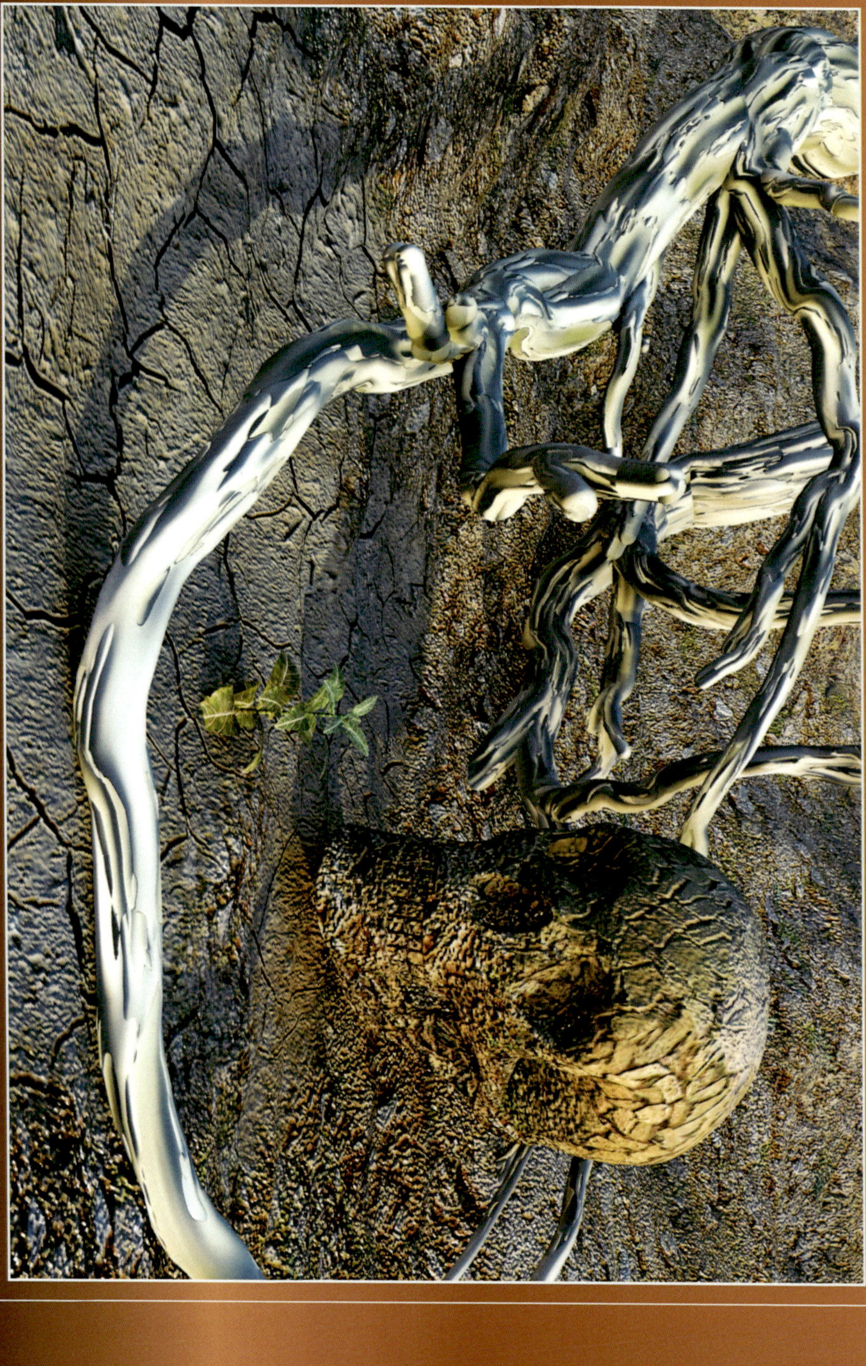

# 9
## ~ Earth ~

*"Work with me through times of uncertainty or change to feel rooted and connected; do not judge yourself or others so harshly"*

What deep rooted beliefs am I digging out? And what beautiful new beliefs am I planting in their place?

What miracles have blessed my life?

How can I best nurture my ideas?

### Affirmations

"As I get to the root, I find sustenance and the promise of growth. I believe miracles can and do happen."

"I experience stability, security and strength of purpose, in this new phase."

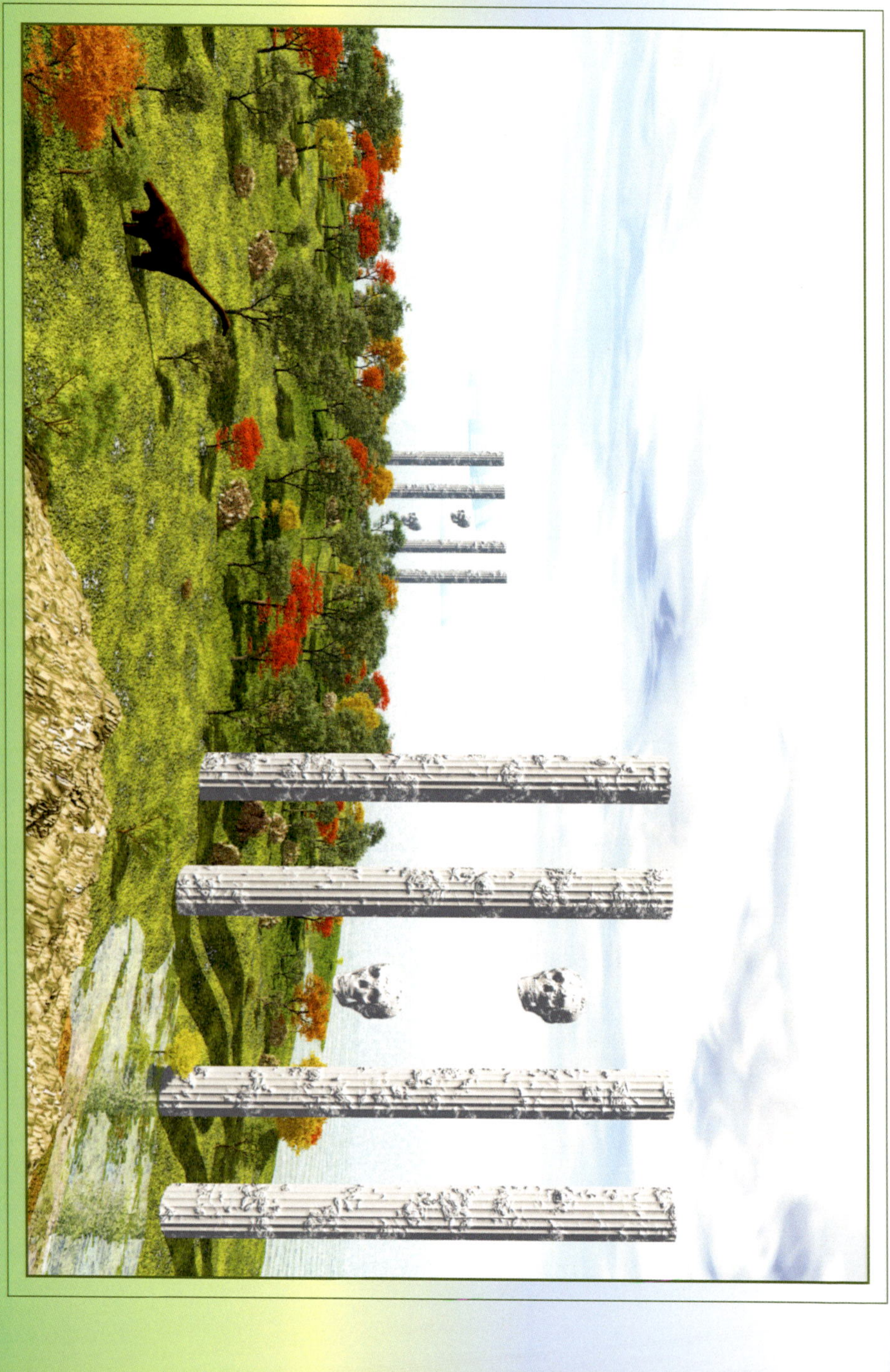

# 10
## ⁓ 11:11 Rebirth ⁓

*"Working with us in the physical and emotional bodies can help bring strength through change"*

Where are my stellar or prehistoric origins?

How best can I transform in this moment to support my future growth?

What opportunities come through rebirth?

### Affirmations

"I access, acknowledge, accept and embrace my origins."

"I allow all energy bodies to be in harmony and all chakras to be in alignment."

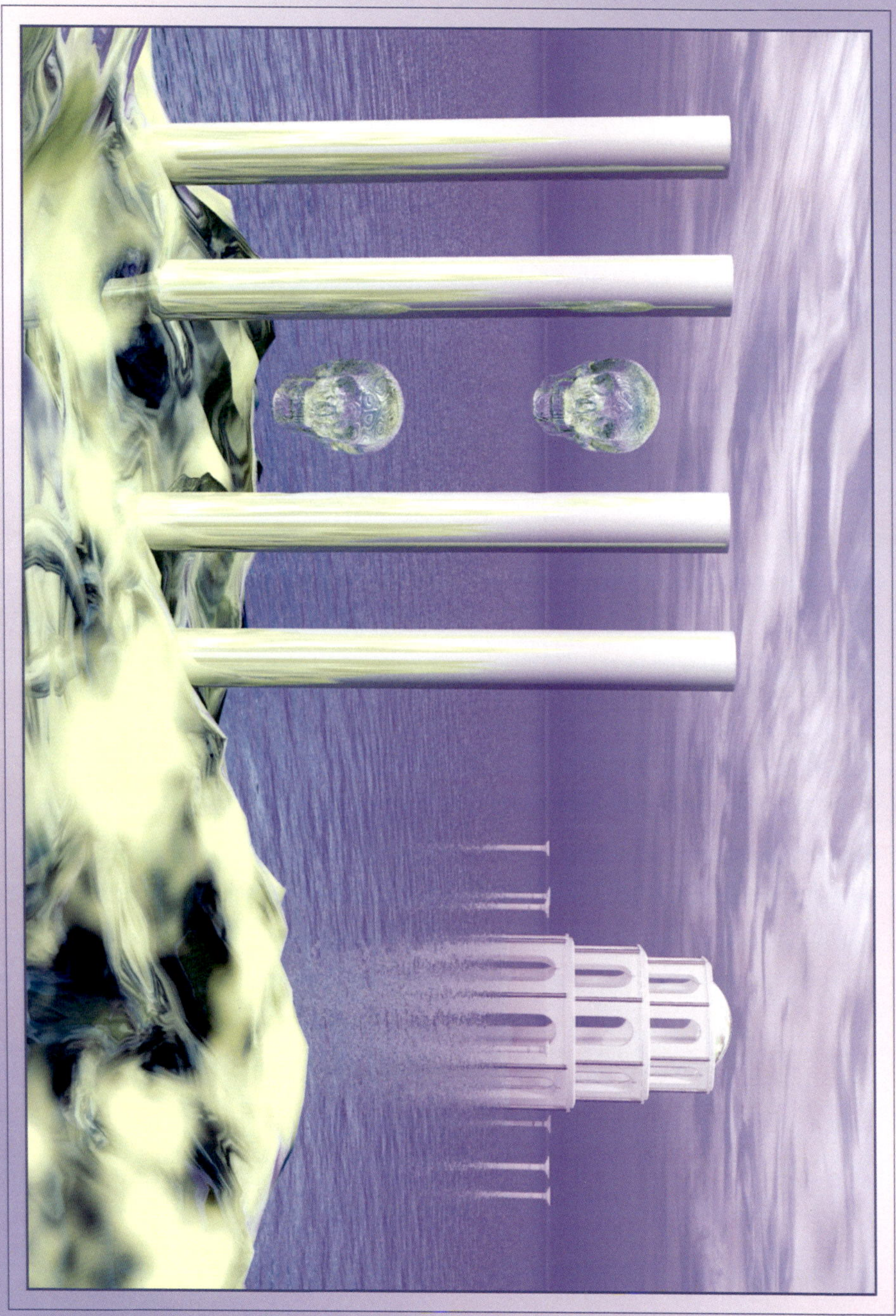

# 11
## ঌ 11:11 Transformation ঌ

*"Work with us to stimulate beautiful & visual meditations and instil a sense of deep peace whilst accessing this state"*

What great personal spiritual transformation is happening?

In what ways am I connected with Atlantis?

How is numerology beneficial to my life and what is it telling me?

### Affirmations

"I am ready, willing and able to embrace an amazing spiritual shift."

"I awaken to my innate healing abilities and allow a deeper understanding of esoteric & evolutionary ideas to flow through me."

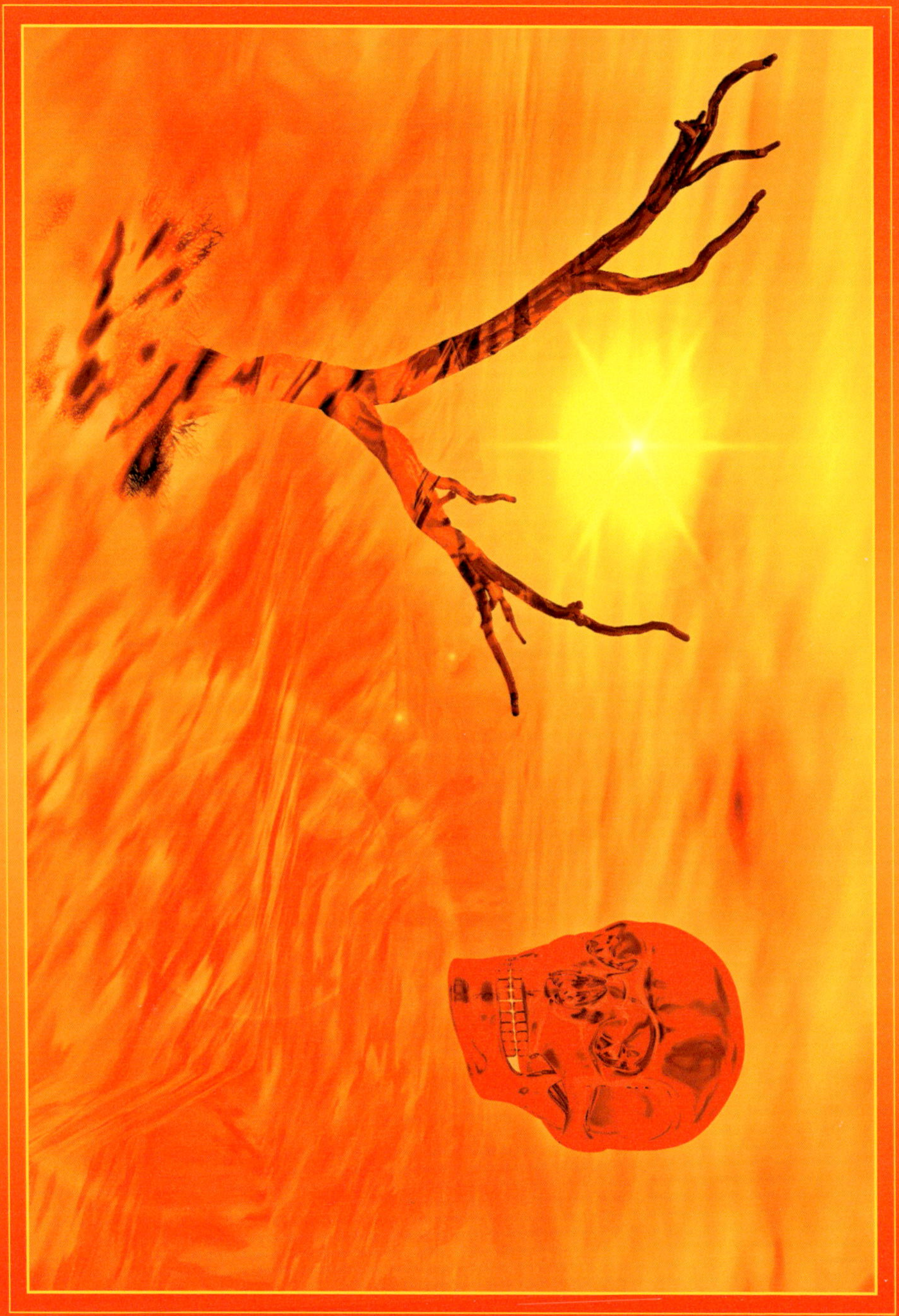

# 12
## ❦ Fire ❦

*"Work with me at the base, sacral & solar plexus to help instil passion, motivation, excitement, creativity & joy"*

What actions must I take now to clear the 'dead wood' from my life?

How can I reignite the passion of intimate relationships?

What dreams inspire me?

### Affirmations

"I take action, reclaim my dreams and rekindle my passion for the things I really desire."

"I allow my path to be cleared so I can move forward in a positive way."

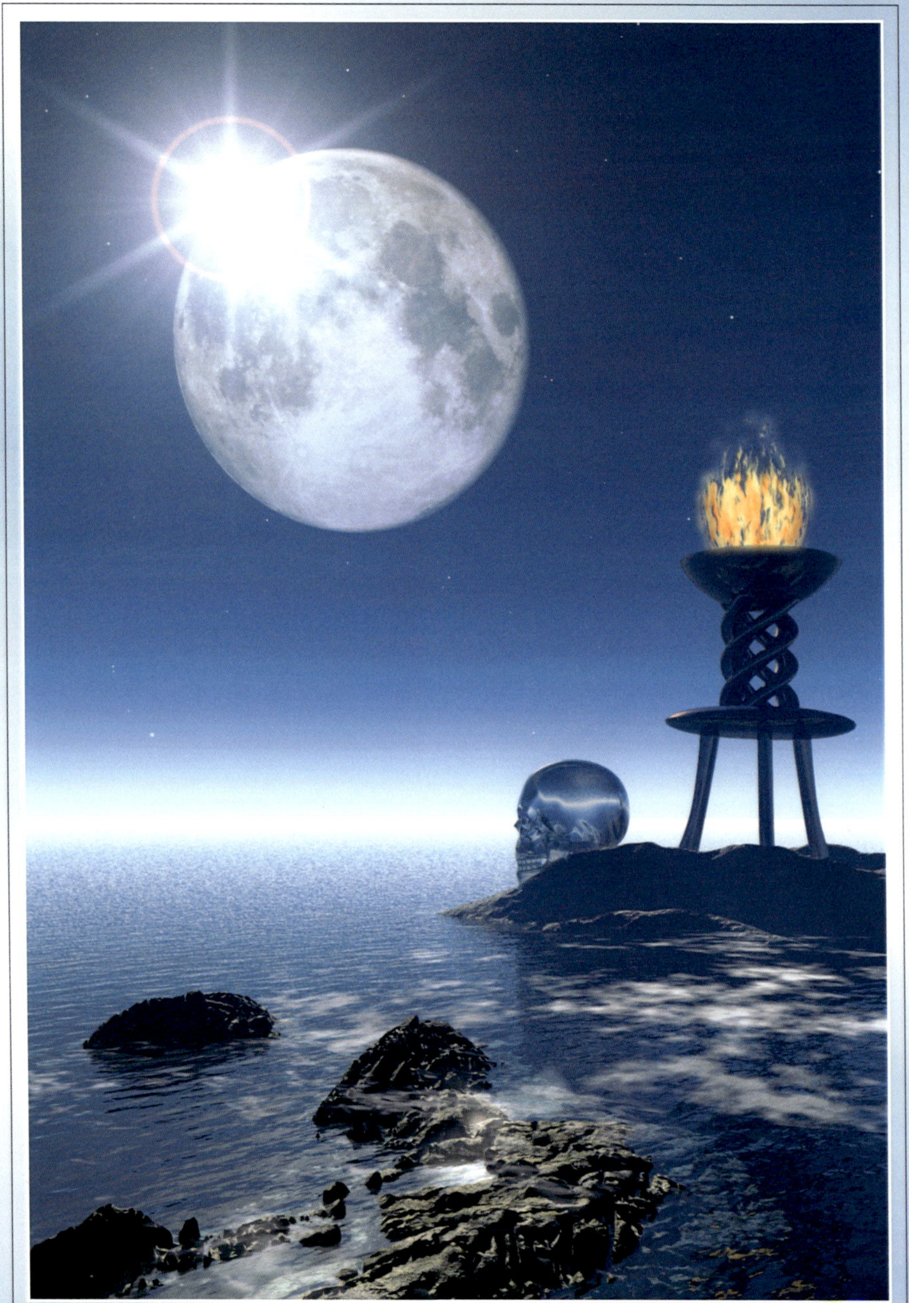

# 13
## ⁓ Guiding Lights ⁓

*"Work with me to bring creative ideas forward so they can be acted upon and communicated to the world"*

How can I move off the sidelines and joyfully participate in life?

What light, dream or opportunity must I follow now?

How amazing can life be when I just take action?

### Affirmations

*"I am grabbing my dream and taking the necessary steps to make it happen!"*

*"I am eager and ready to learn now, as I have clarity of mind & emotions."*

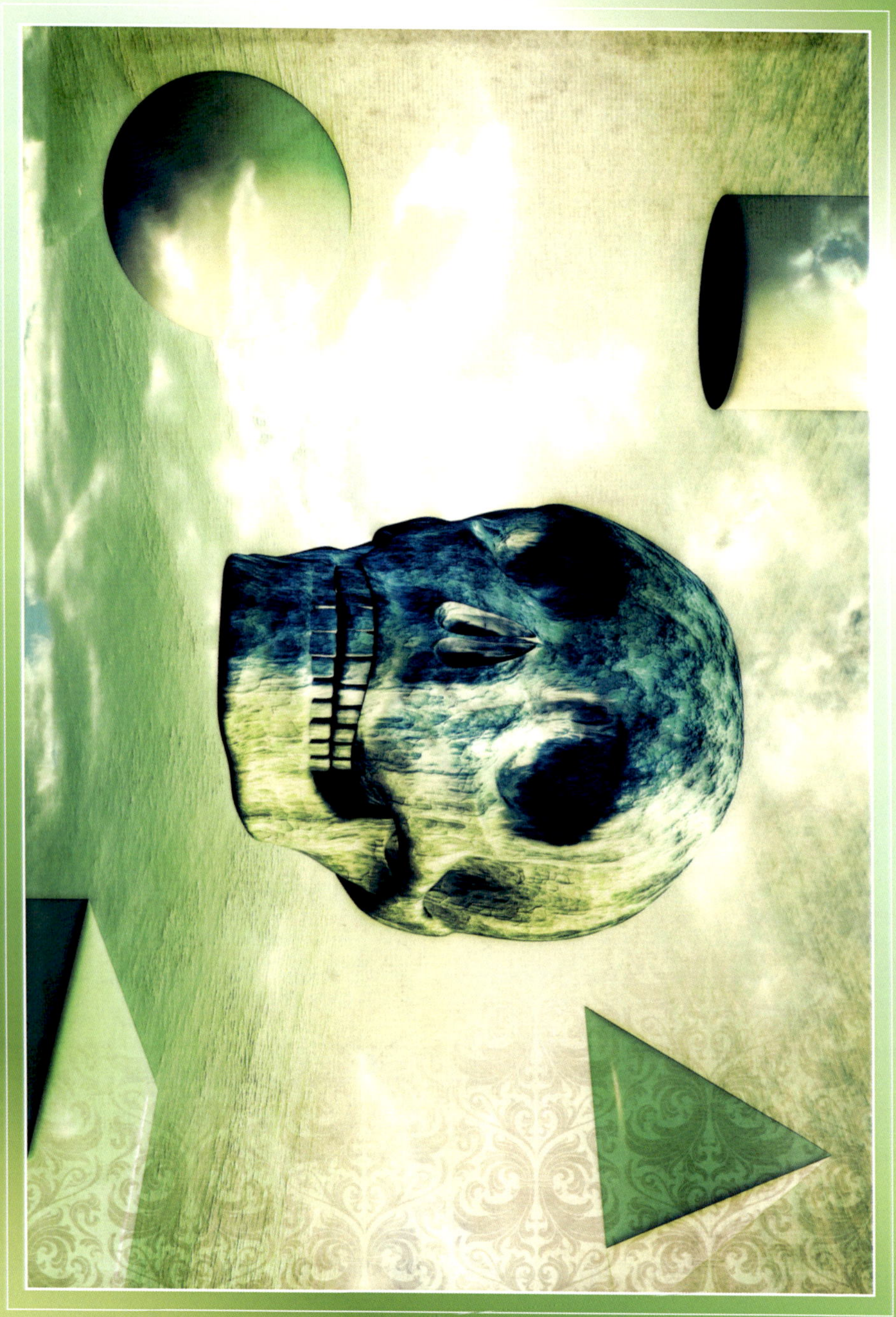

# 14
## ∾ Imagination ∾

*"Work with me to energise your heart and throat bringing confidence to share your imagination with the world"*

How is my imagination more important than my knowledge?

Which beautiful idea am I most committed to bringing to fruition?

In what ways could I make my ideas bigger and better?

---

### Affirmations

"I can picture something truly amazing and I can bring it to life."

"Imagination is a building block of life. I am starting today, one block at a time."

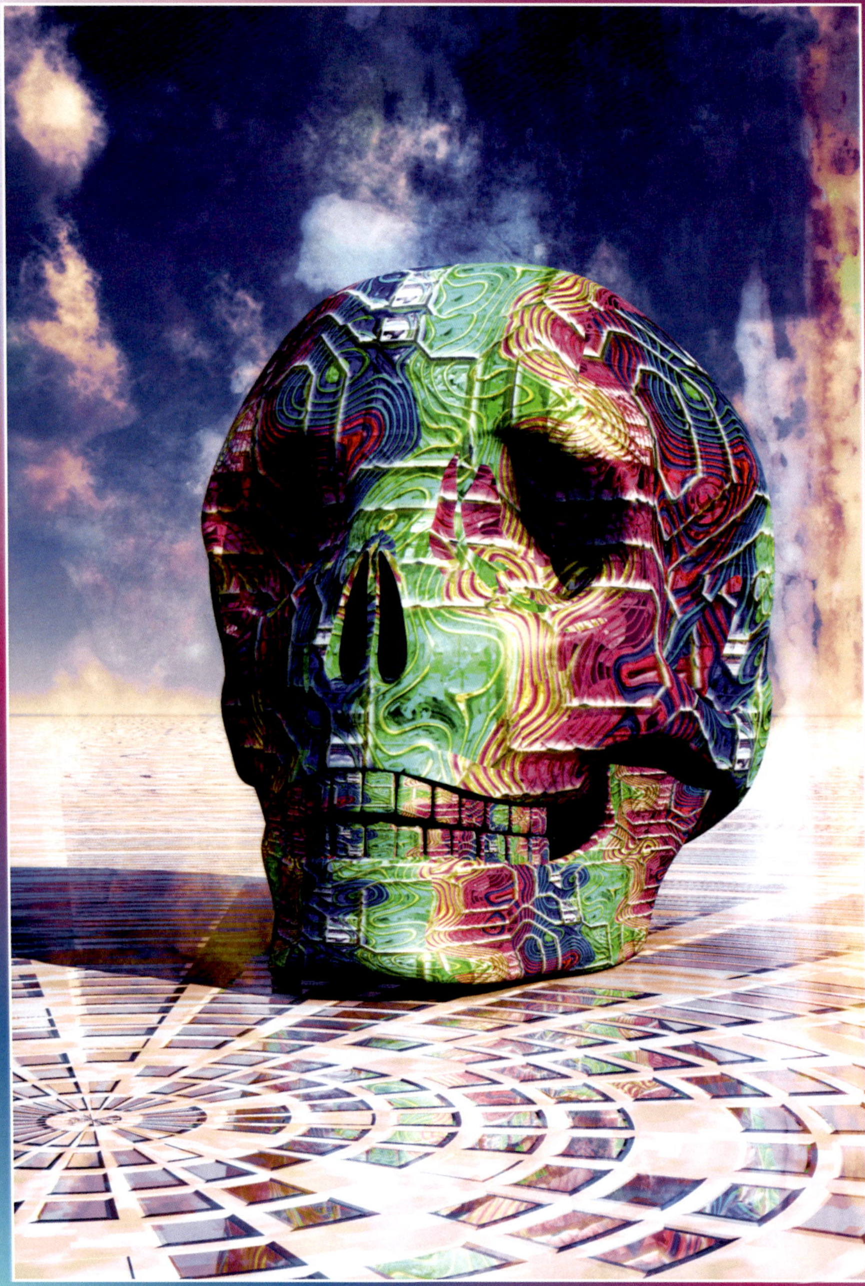

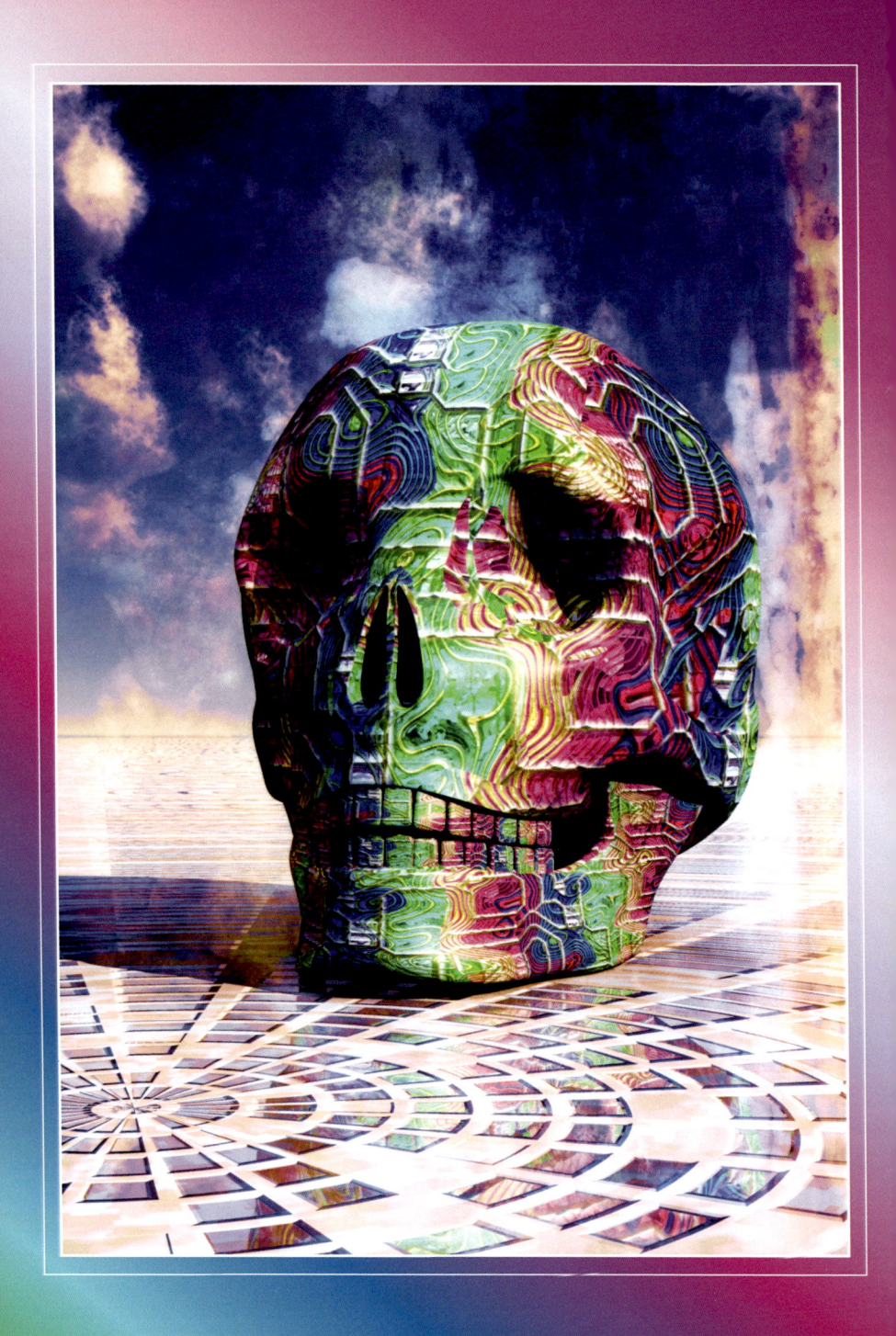

# 15
## ❧ Individuality ☙

*"Work with me to energise all chakras, and all colours within, for courage & conviction to communicate from the heart"*

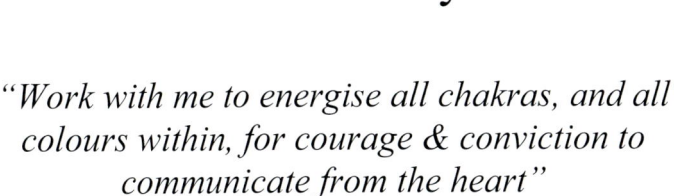

Where do I find the courage to stand in my 'youniqueness'?

How do I celebrate the ways I am different?

Why is my individuality good for me and the world?

### Affirmations

"I stand in the power of my 'youniqueness' and share with the world what makes me awesome."

"I understand my mission and I am happy & proud to stand out."

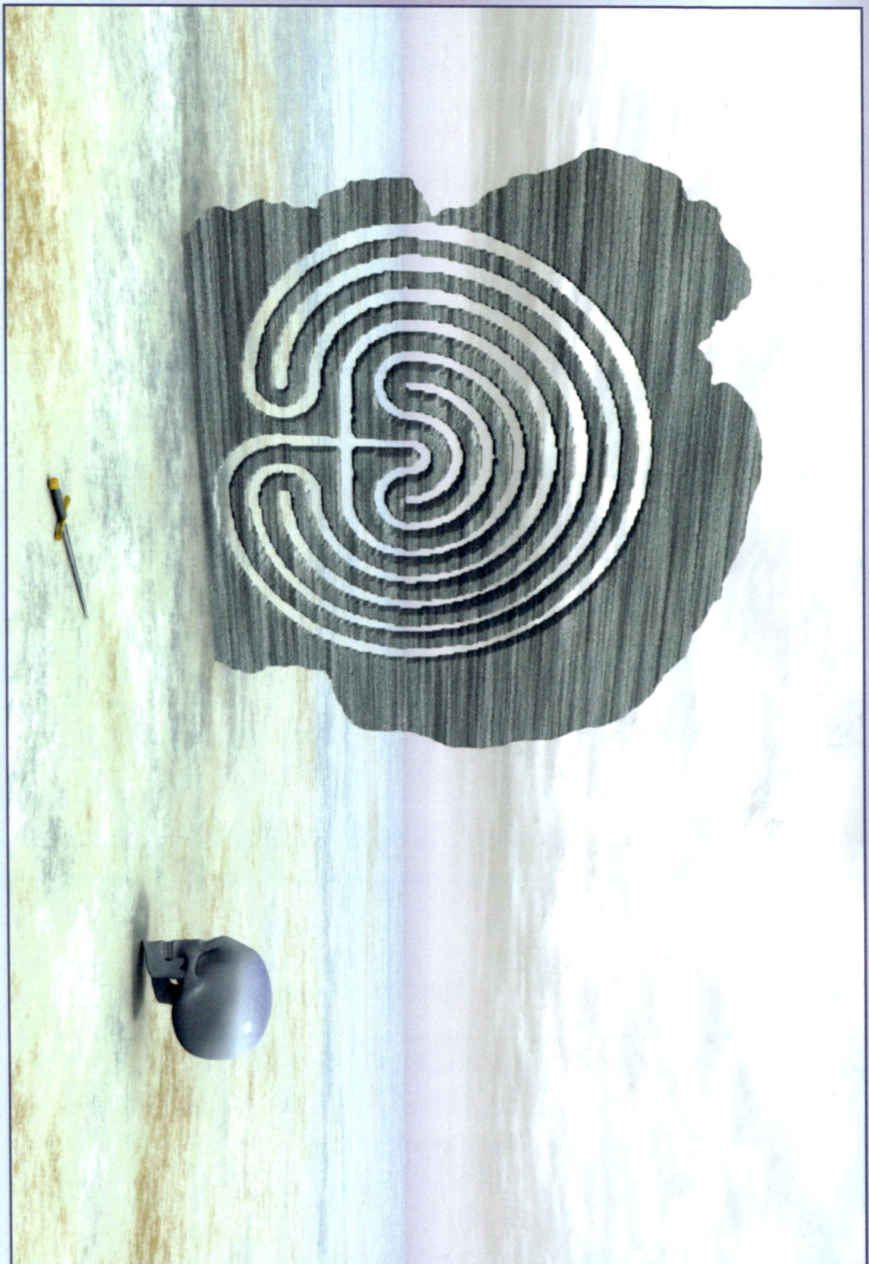

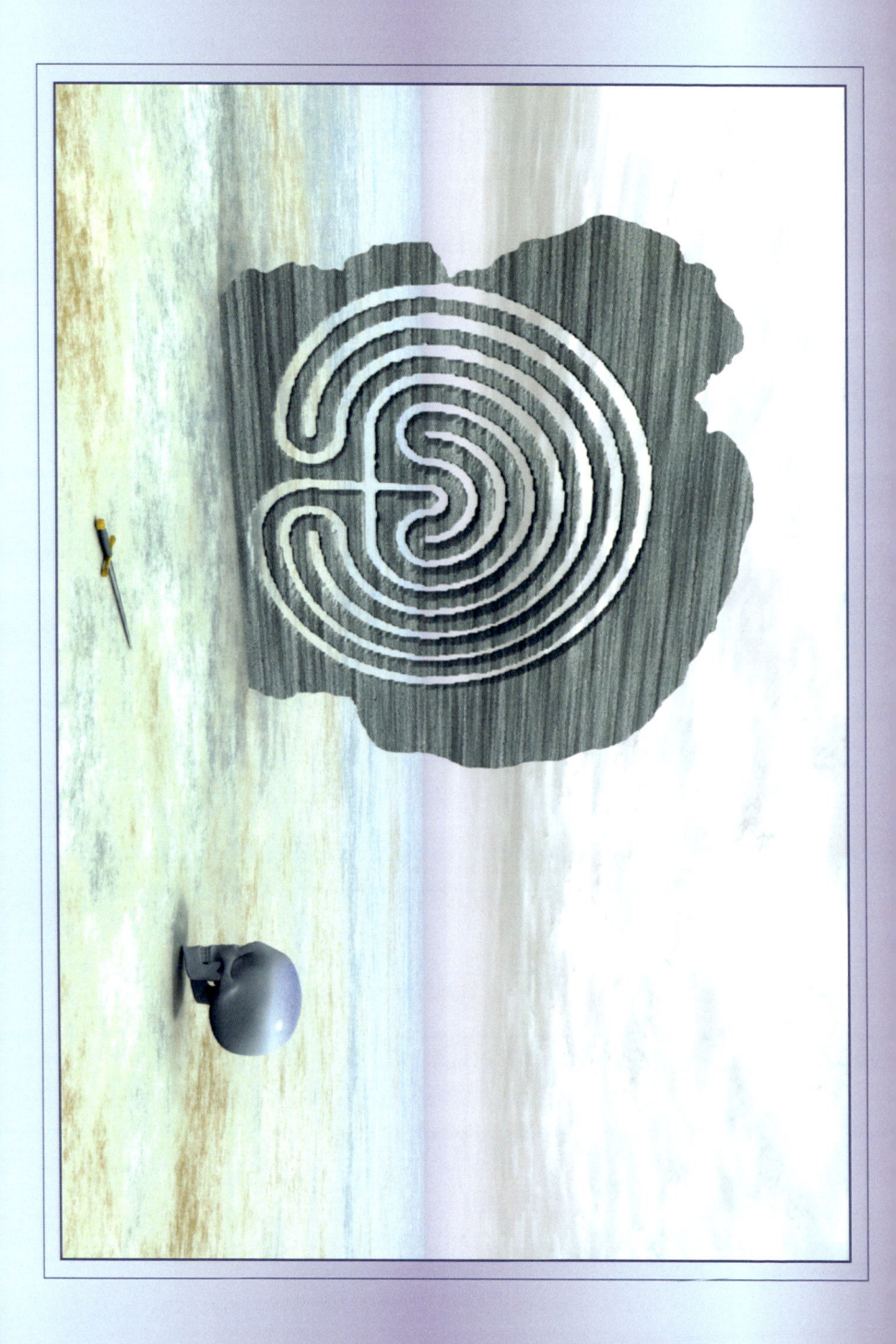

# 16
## ◈ Labyrinth ◈

*"Work with me to help bring a sense of calm to all aspects of mind, body and soul. Lay down your sword; stop fighting"*

Where does my mind need to be focused right now?

What can 'walking a Labyrinth' do for me?

How can accessing different dimensions or parallel lives help me?

### Affirmations

"I walk the Labyrinth in my mind and experience an amazing new dimension."

"Through cleansing, clarity and deep peace, I access the 'real truth' of All That Is."

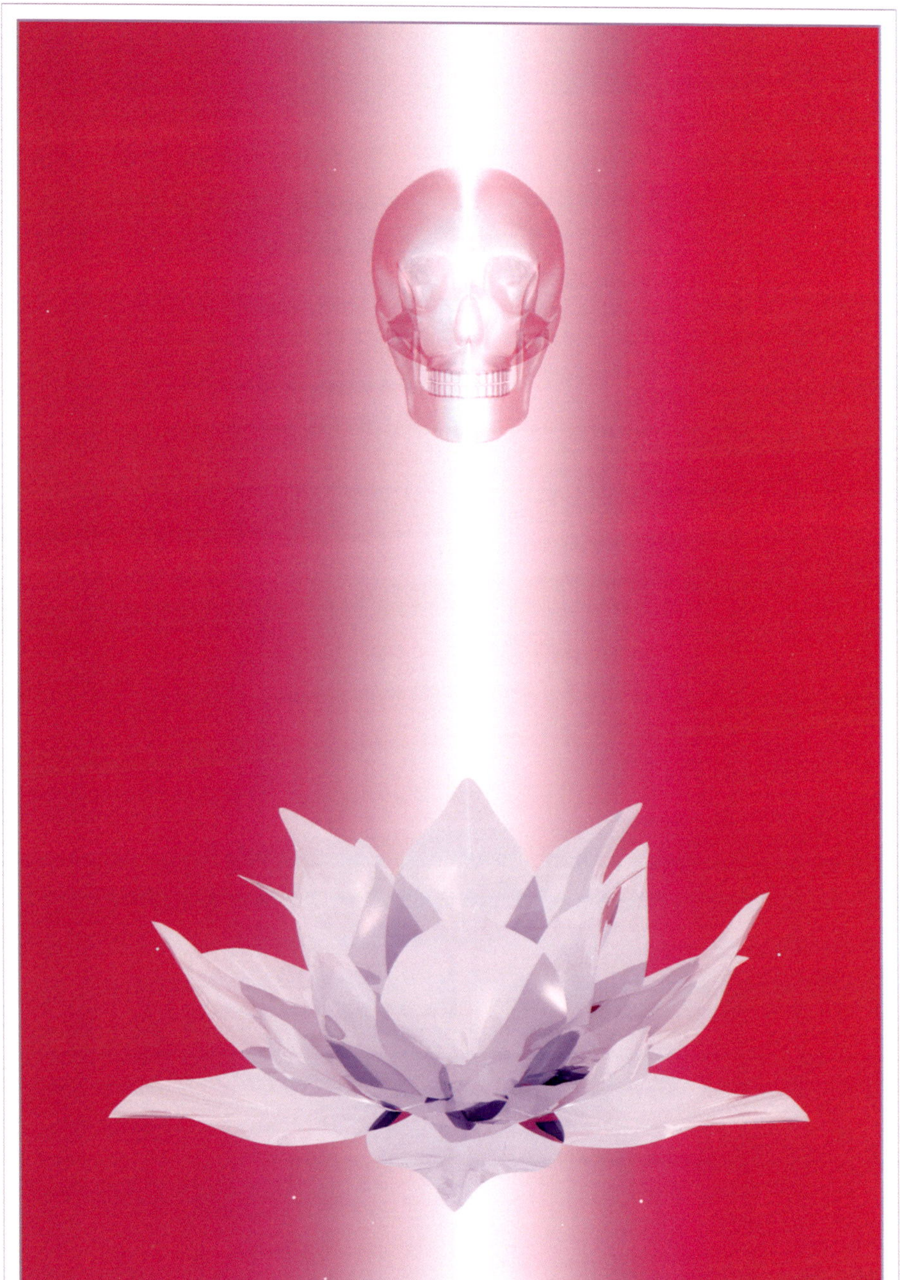

# 17
## ✥ Lotus Flower ✥

*"Work with me after a period of
depression or confusion
as I am both soothing and energising"*

How could I take the things I find challenging and make them effortless?

How can I bring more 'sunshine' into my life?

What old behaviours no longer serve me? And what new behaviours will I adopt instead?

### Affirmations

*"I am open to experiencing a transformation of beauty and perfection."*

*"I allow myself to let go of the old with ease as I embrace heightened creativity and Divine Love."*

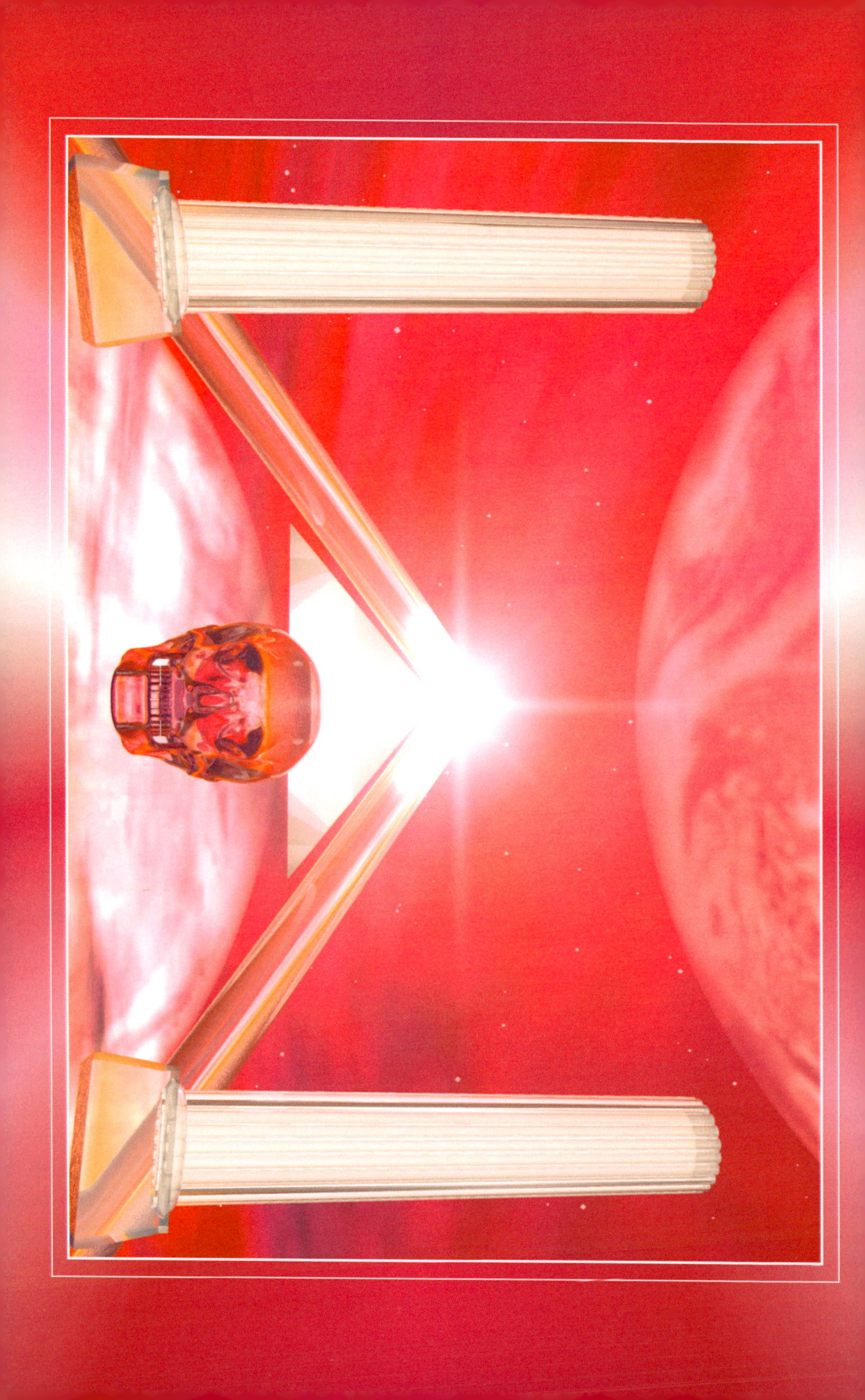

# 18
## ༄ Magenta Bridge ༄

*"Work with me to help activate your soul star, crown, heart and sacral"*

Why did I choose to incarnate on Earth at this time?

How can I stay connected with my 'off world' home?

What wisdom, creativity and teachings do I need to share with the world?

### Affirmations

"I understand my purpose. I bring healing and enlightenment through staying connected with my home."

"I am exactly where I am supposed to be. My presence and actions help to raise the vibrations and collective consciousness of humanity."

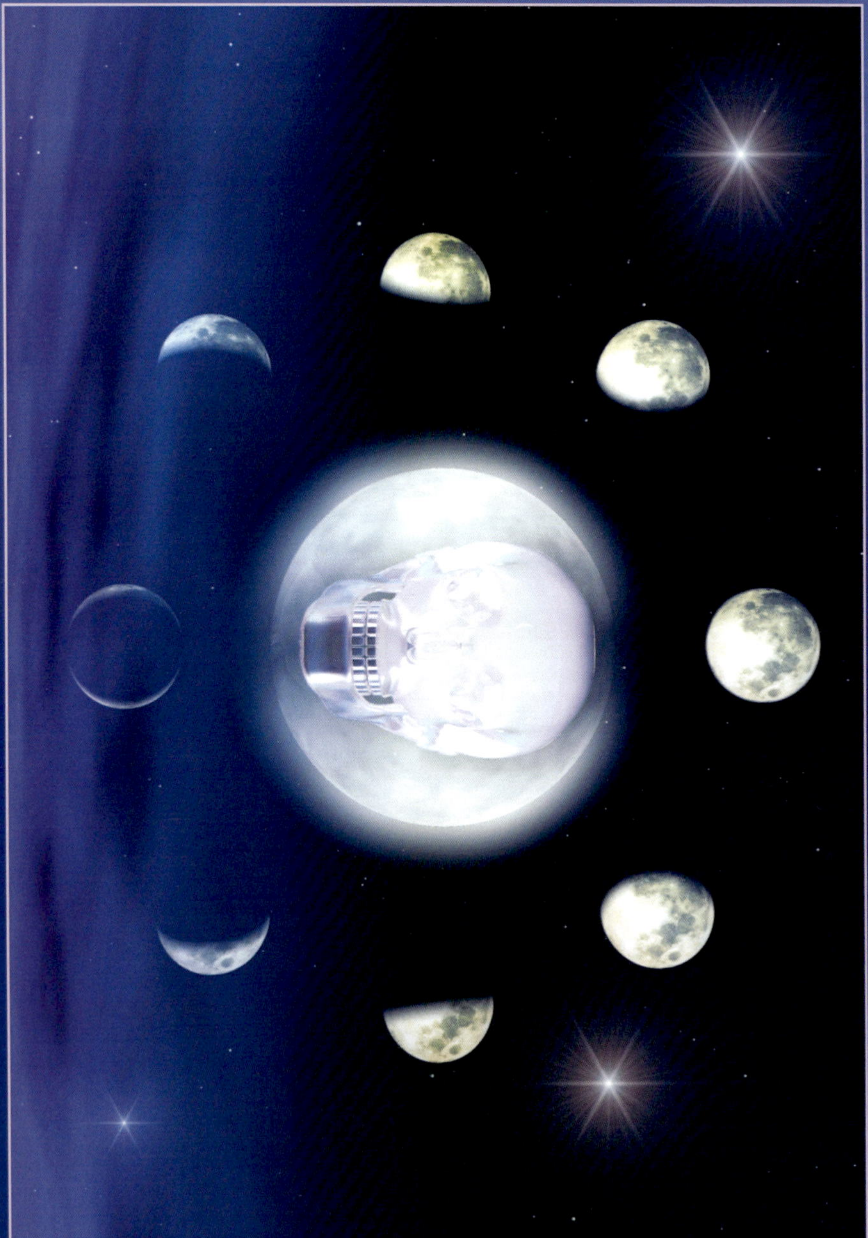

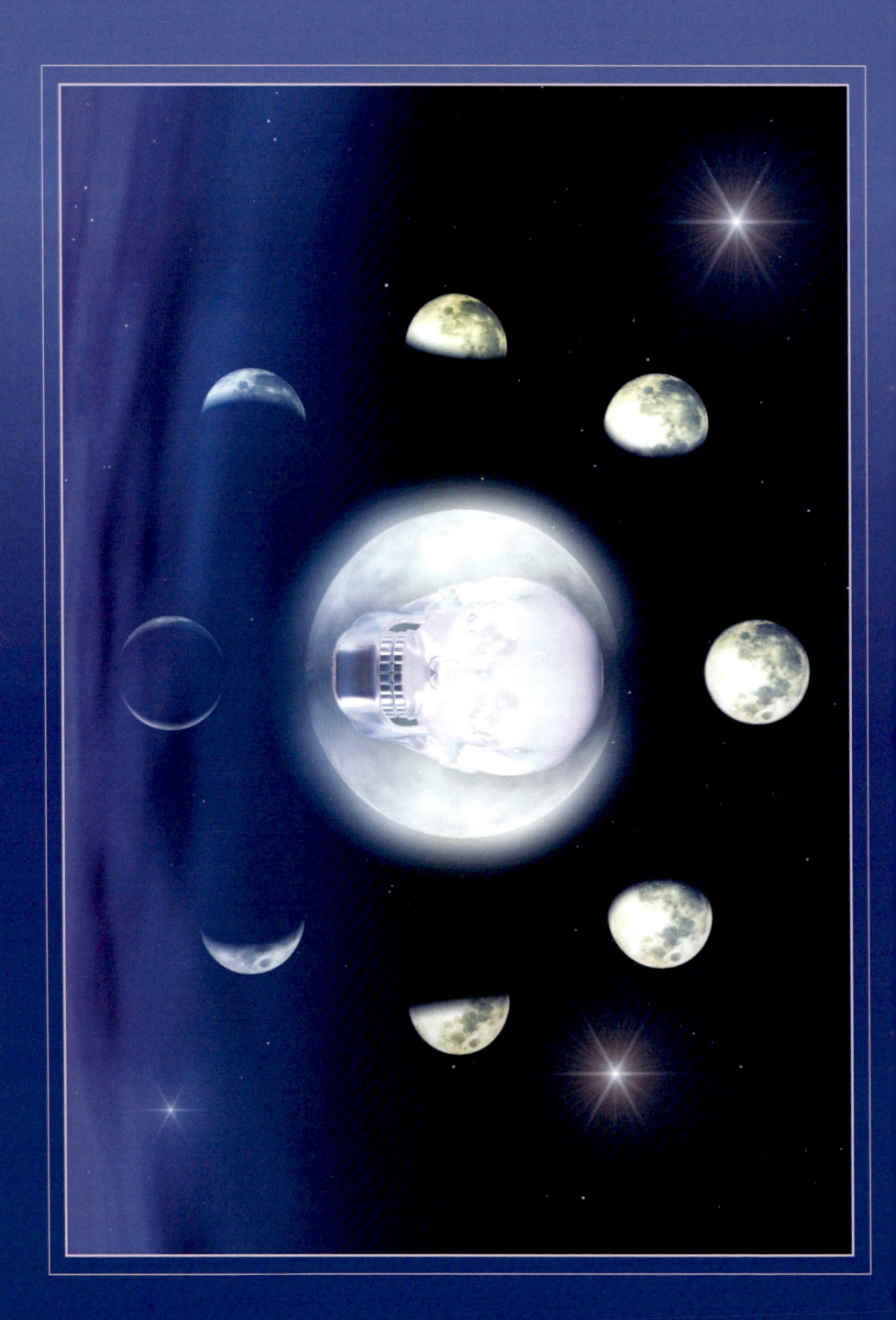

# 19
## ৩ Moon Phases ৯

*"Work with me to help bring clarity, inspiration & healing and to activate the third eye, throat & crown chakra"*

How can Moon energy help me at this time? And in what creative ways can I tap into this energy?

Which crystals need cleansing right now?

Am I in a renewal, creation or wisdom phase? And how can I benefit fully from this?

---

### Affirmations

*"I easily access deep, meditative states that unleash my creativity and bring inspiring visions for the future."*

*"My emotions are calm as I experience serenity and go with the flow."*

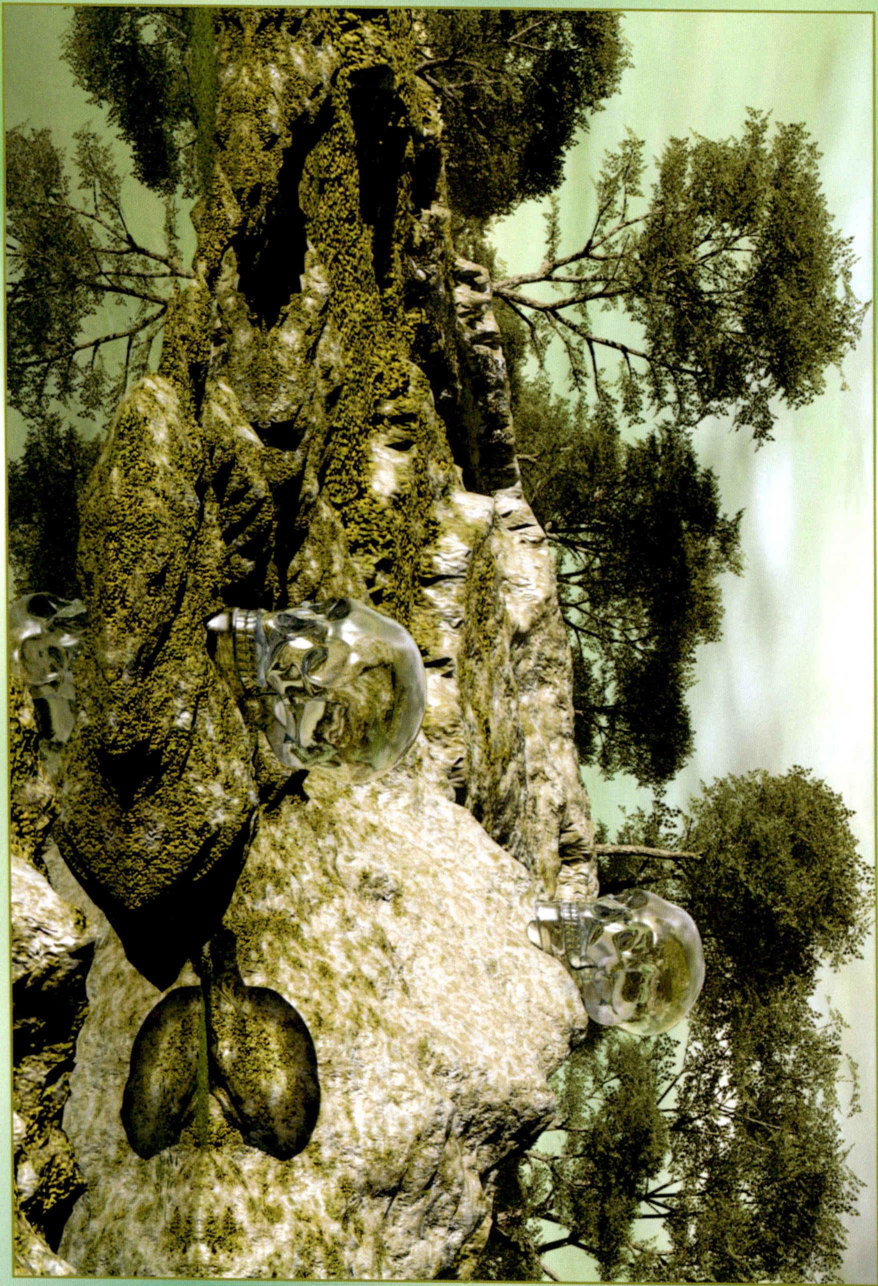

# 20
## ∽ Nature ∾

*"Work with us as we assist in connecting you with Mother Earth, which can help regulate and strengthen the heartbeat"*

Where should I go to rest and regenerate?

What do the birds, bees and butterflies have to tell me? And how can I integrate these lessons?

How can I make the best use of flowers, herbs and natural plant remedies?

### Affirmations

"I stop to take a breath that fills my lungs, heart and soul with the life force that surrounds me."

"I invite new beginnings and appreciate Nature for all the wonders it continues to bring me."

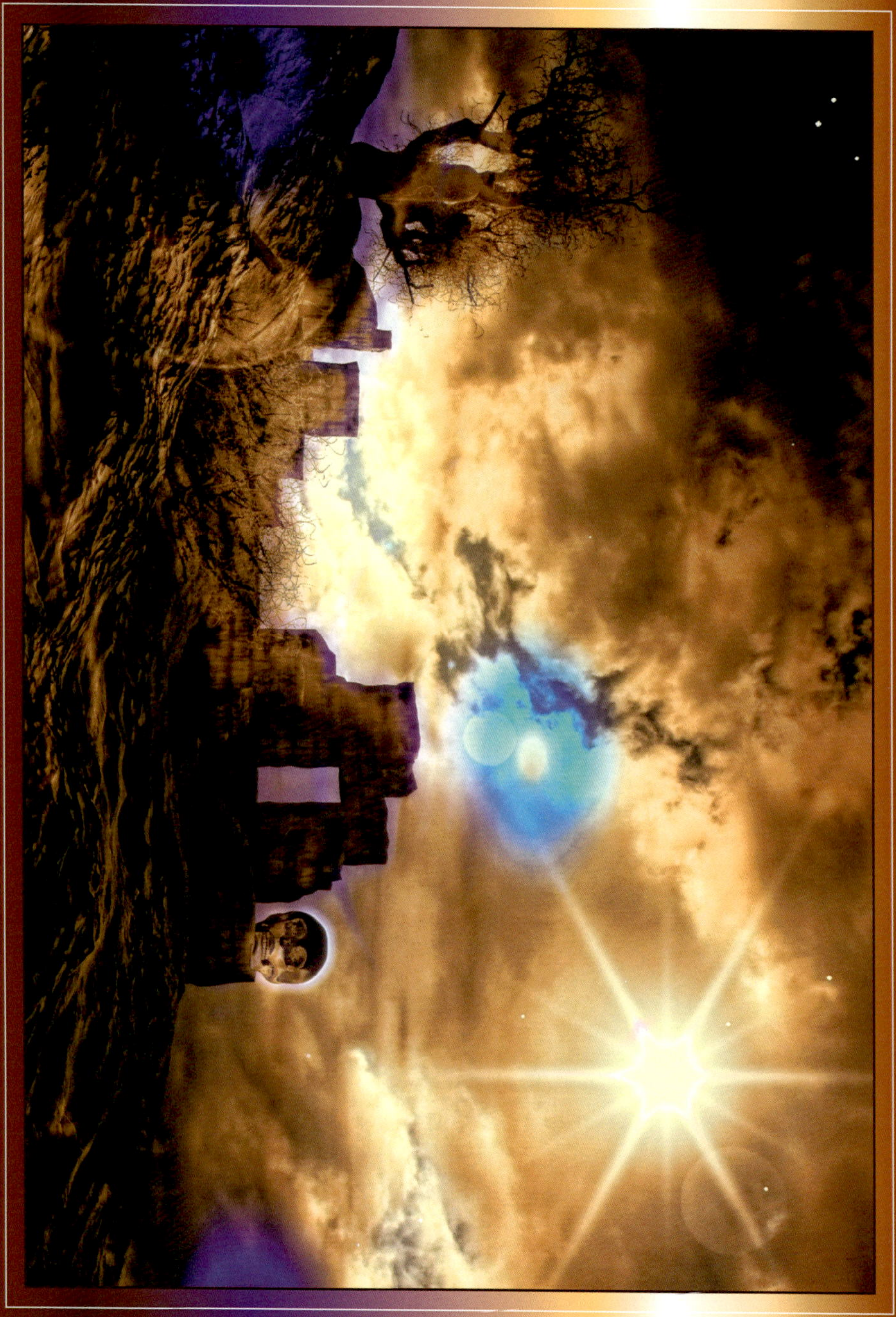

# 21
## ∽ Perception ∾

*"Work with me to energise the base, third eye and crown for manifestation of new beginnings"*

How does changing my perspective, change my possibilities?

What potential can I see for beautiful creation, development and growth?

How much light is within and around me?

### Affirmations

"Now I am facing the right direction, I see things differently. My fabulous foundations are just being laid."

"I see the light bursting through and I am now full of new possibilities."

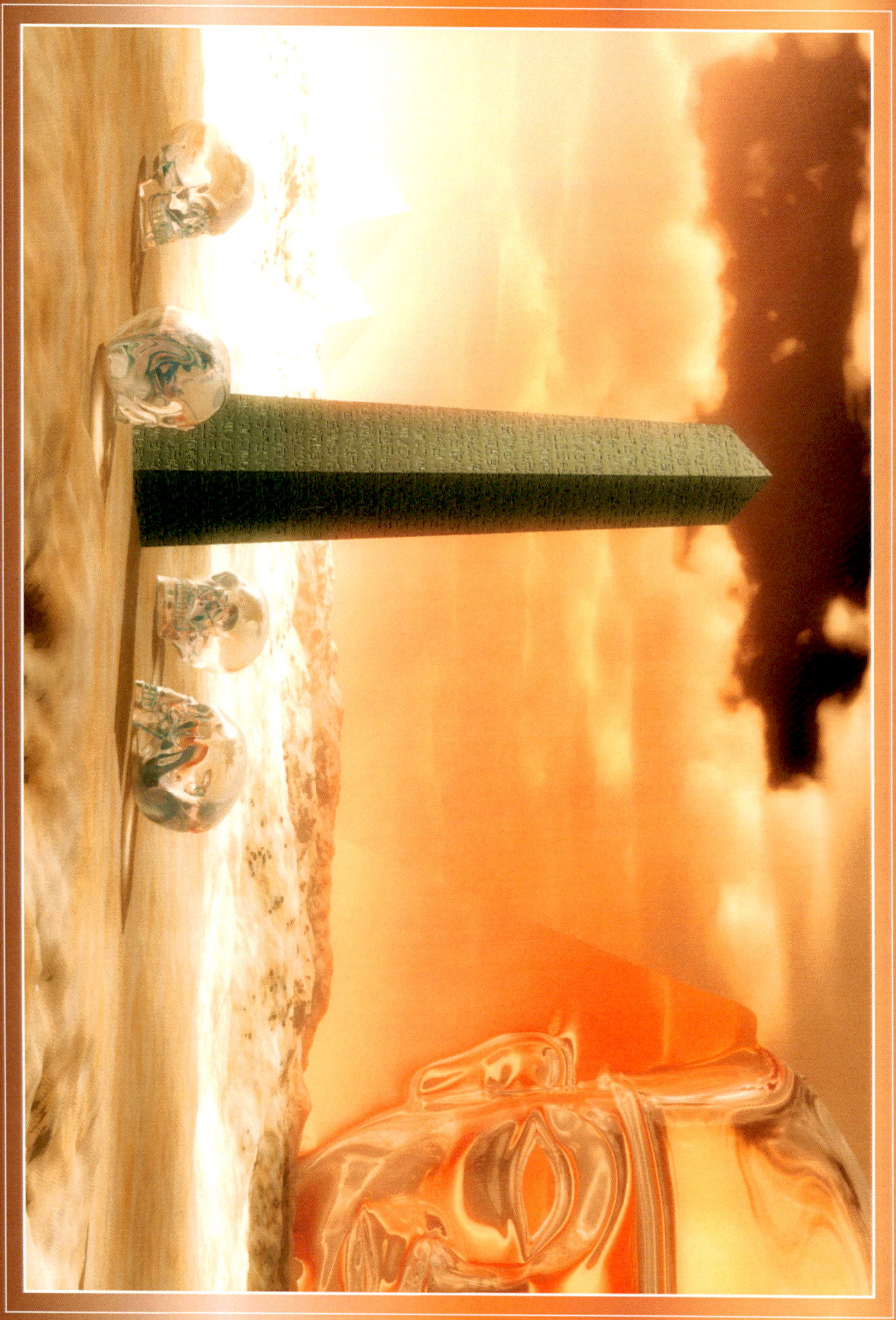

## 22
### ꙮ Obelisk ꙮ

*"Work with us to energise the creative sacral centre and no longer be afraid. Don't allow your messages to be compromised"*

What could I learn from Greek
and Egyptian mythology?

How best can I express my inspirations,
thoughts and feelings?

What information do I need to share at this time?
And how am I going to share it?

### Affirmations

"I am safe and protected as I make
my connections."

"I am excited to be a channel for
poetry, automatic writing
and inspirational messages."

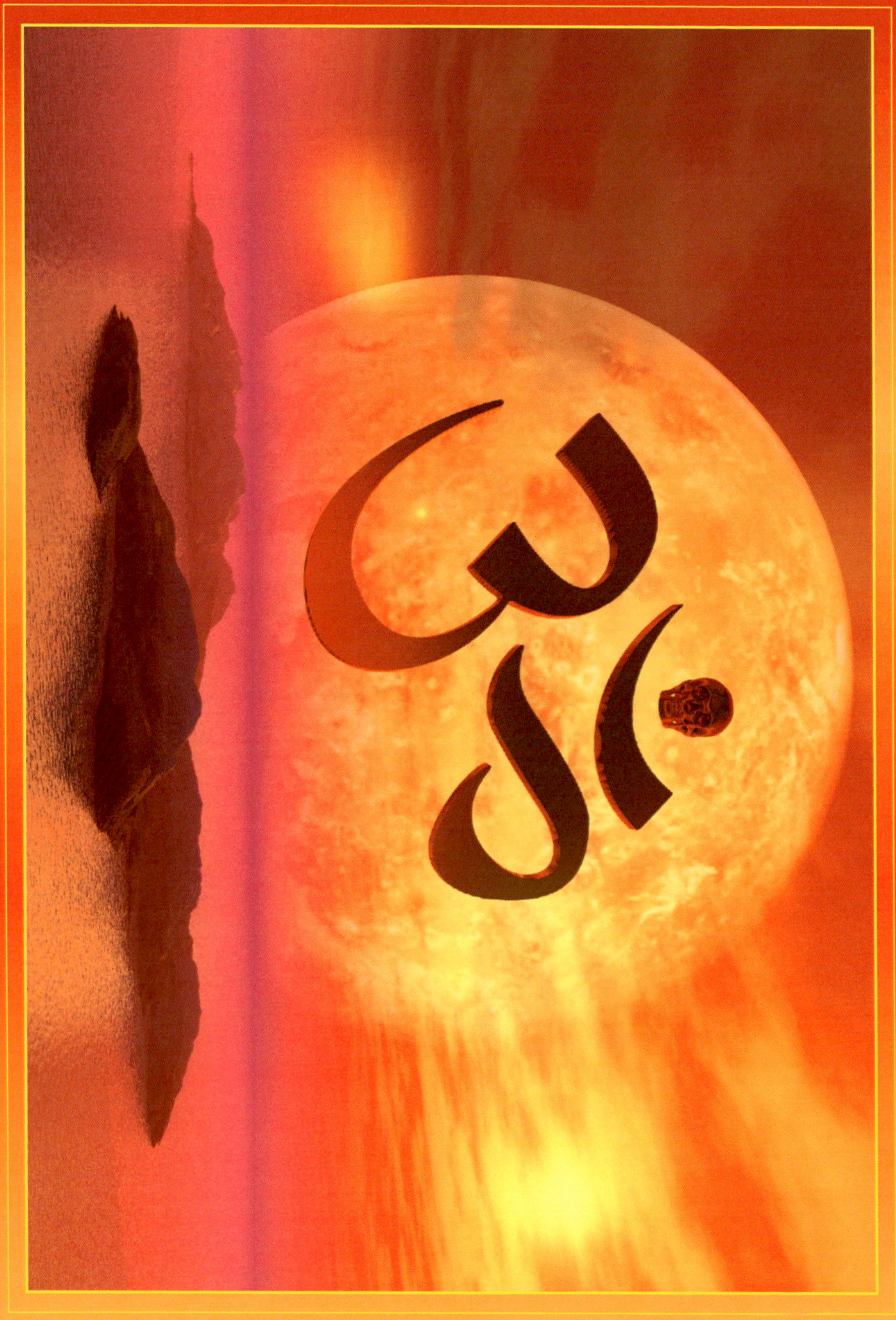

# 23
## ∽ Om ∾

*"Work with me to instil a sense of passion, excitement, joy, motivation & creativity especially for music and sound"*

How can I use the power of sound to tap into my inner resources and creativity?

What Tibetan connections do I have?

What does Mother Earth sound like to me?

## Affirmations

"I harness the vibrations of the sun and sound to help find my inner sanctuary."

"I draw from the strength of the planet and feel its cleansing, healing & strengthening power flow through me."

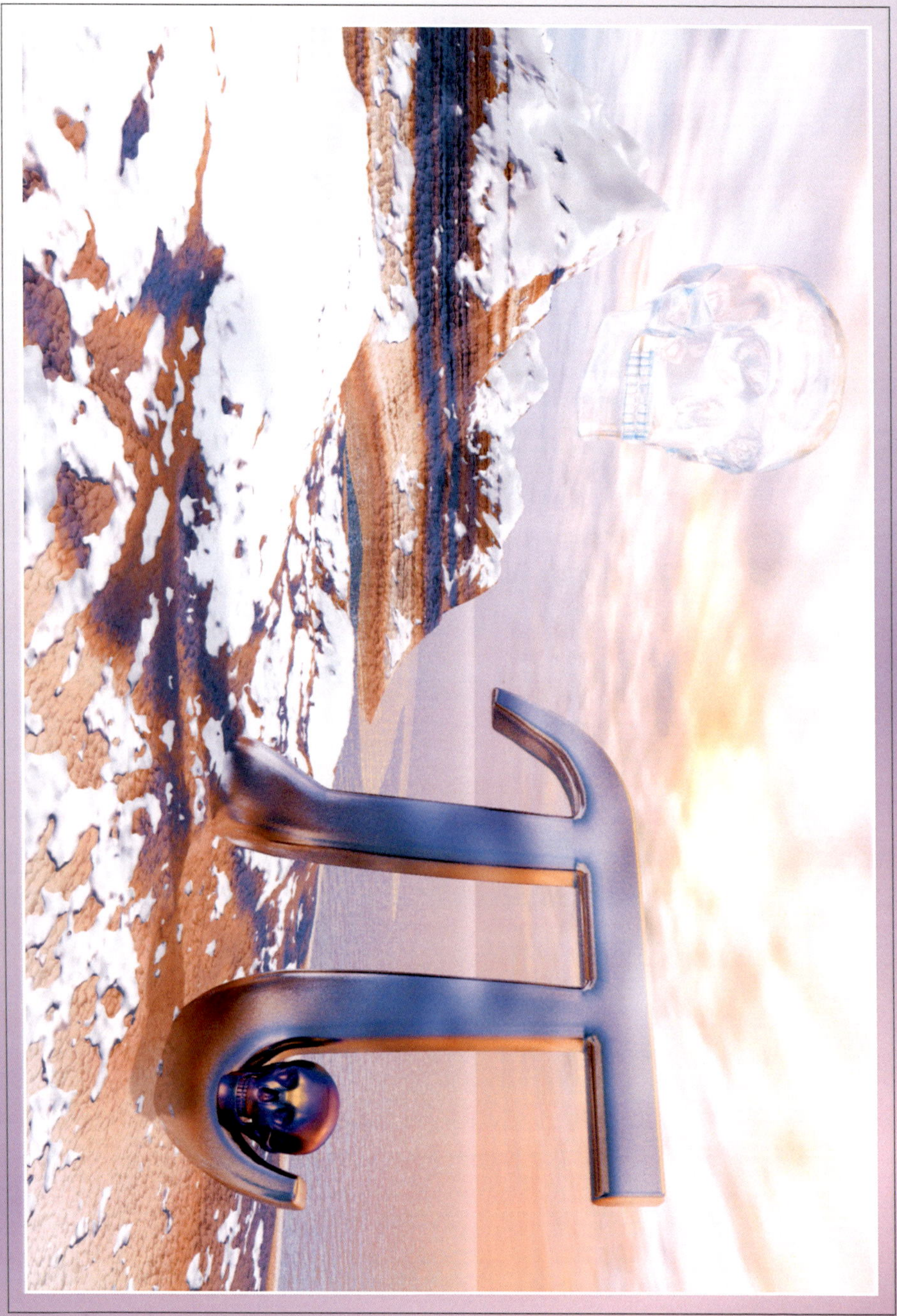

# 24
## ∽ Pi ∾

*"Work with us to bring calm to the solar plexus, especially whilst uncovering layers that might normally make you feel uncomfortable"*

What is the question?

What can I learn from the power of sacred sites?

What would be the benefits of me creating a circle for healing, development or meditation?

### Affirmations

"As I uncover the many amazing layers, I feel balanced and inspired."

"I bathe in the history, significance and healing of sacred sites as they share their truths and power with me."

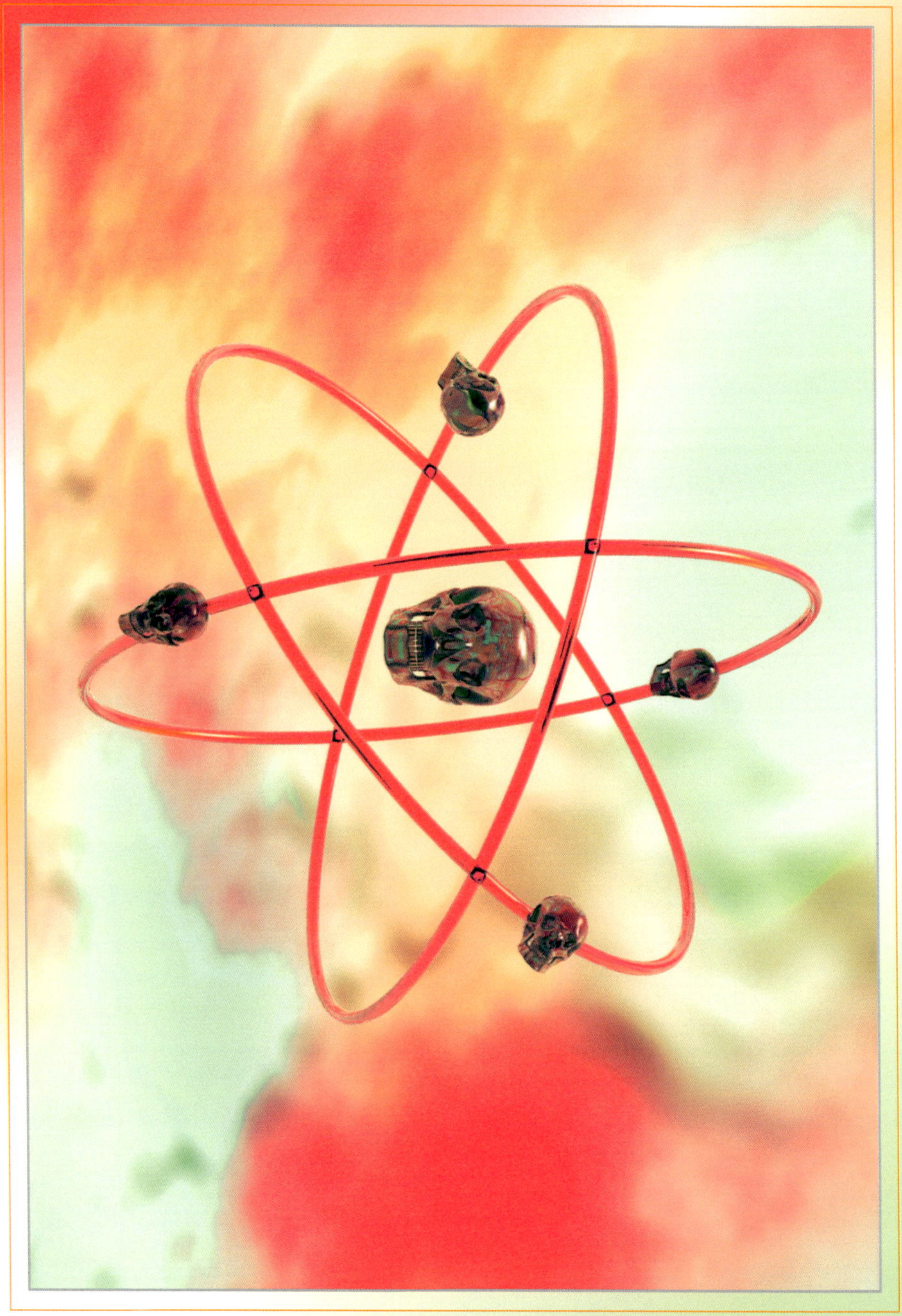

# 25
## ∽ Protection ∾

*"Work with us and our intense vibration of Love; and Love will be your sole/soul experience in any situation"*

What fears are disempowering me? And what action will I take to transmute them into powerful resources?

Am I a counsellor, bridger of worlds or mediator?

How best can I help others overcome their vulnerability?

### Affirmations

"Even in situations of emotional tension, I can communicate effectively with others."

"I feel strong, safe and connected. Love is my protection. I am of Love, I am in Love and I exude Love."

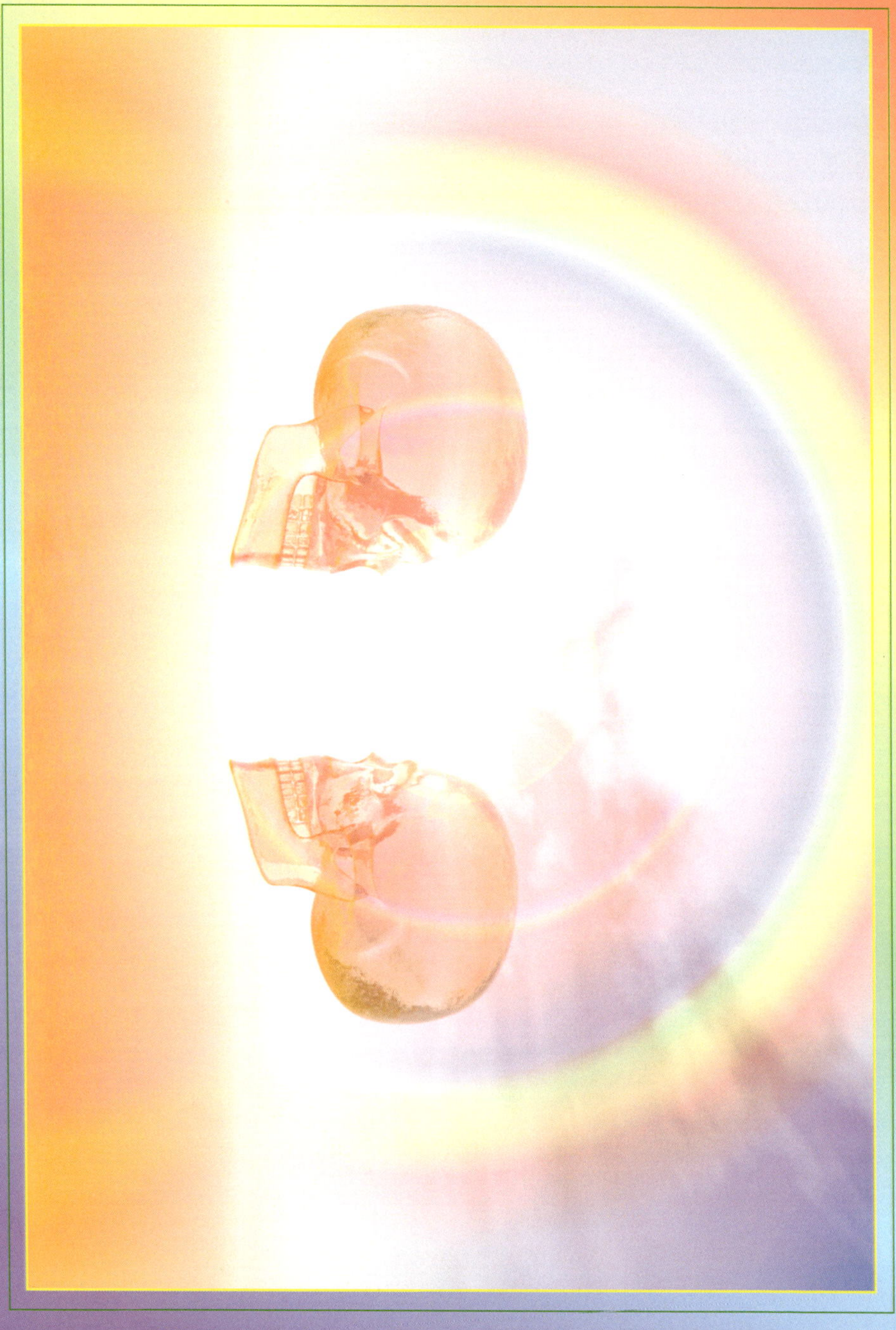

# 26
## ✧ Rainbow ✧

*"Work with us for harmony at whatever level is needed. We can bring calm and energy at the same time"*

Why have I been unhappy? And how can I change my perspective to generate a better feeling?

What does it take to make a Rainbow?

What things bring me the greatest joy in my life?

---

### Affirmations

"I enjoy a complete sense of harmony, beauty, delight and happiness as I embrace the colours of the Rainbow."

"Each time I see a Rainbow in the sky, I know it comes with love from those up high."

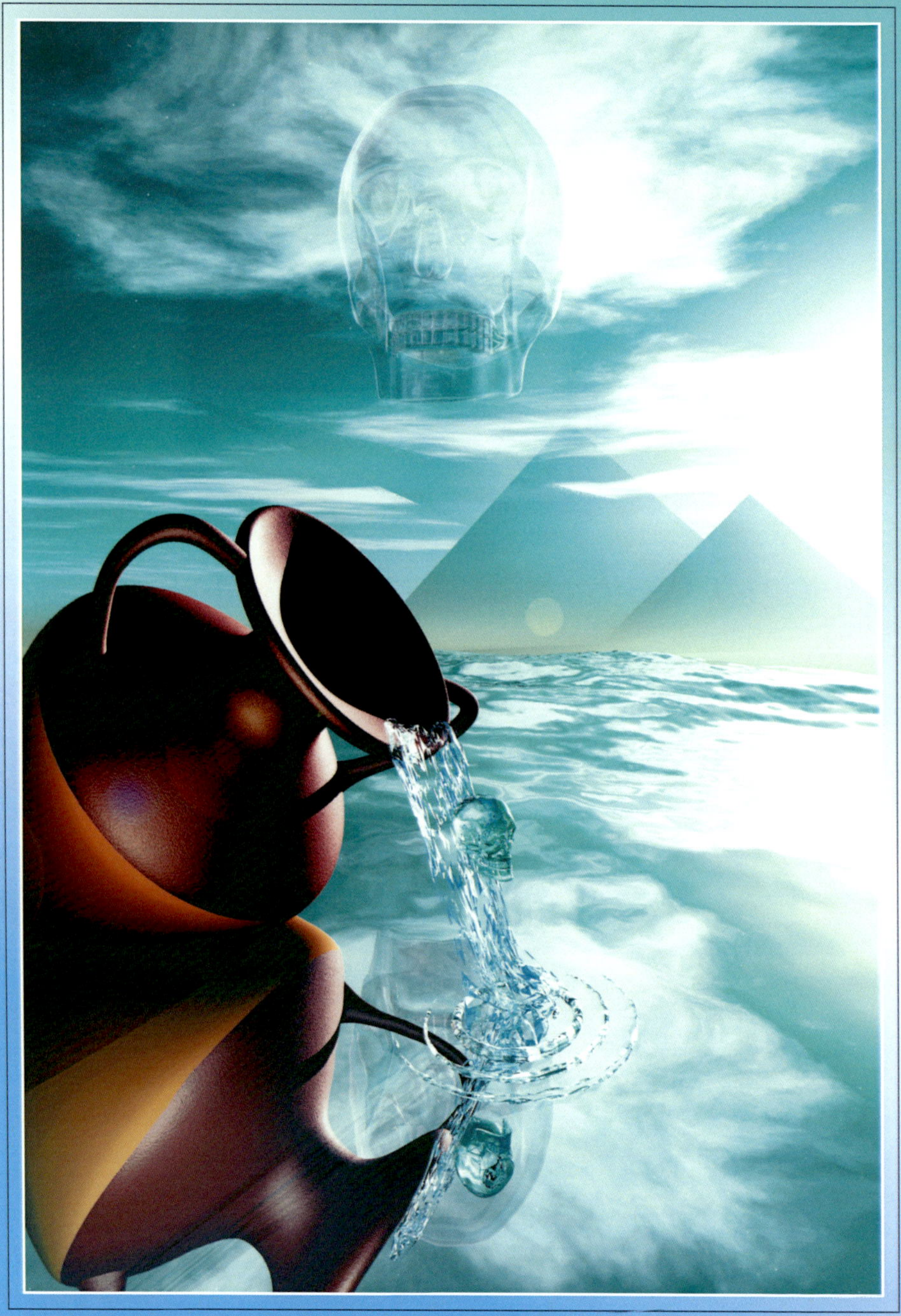

# 27
## ≼ Recycle ≽

*"Work with us to help cleanse the entire auric field and also to activate the base, sacral, throat & crown"*

How can I be as clear a channel as I possibly can be?

What do I need to purify or relearn? And how am I releasing the things that have held me back?

How can I distil complex teachings to make them truly useful?

### Affirmations

"As the energy of the universe flows through me, I release and recycle."

"I feel cleansed and inspired; full of peace and clarity."

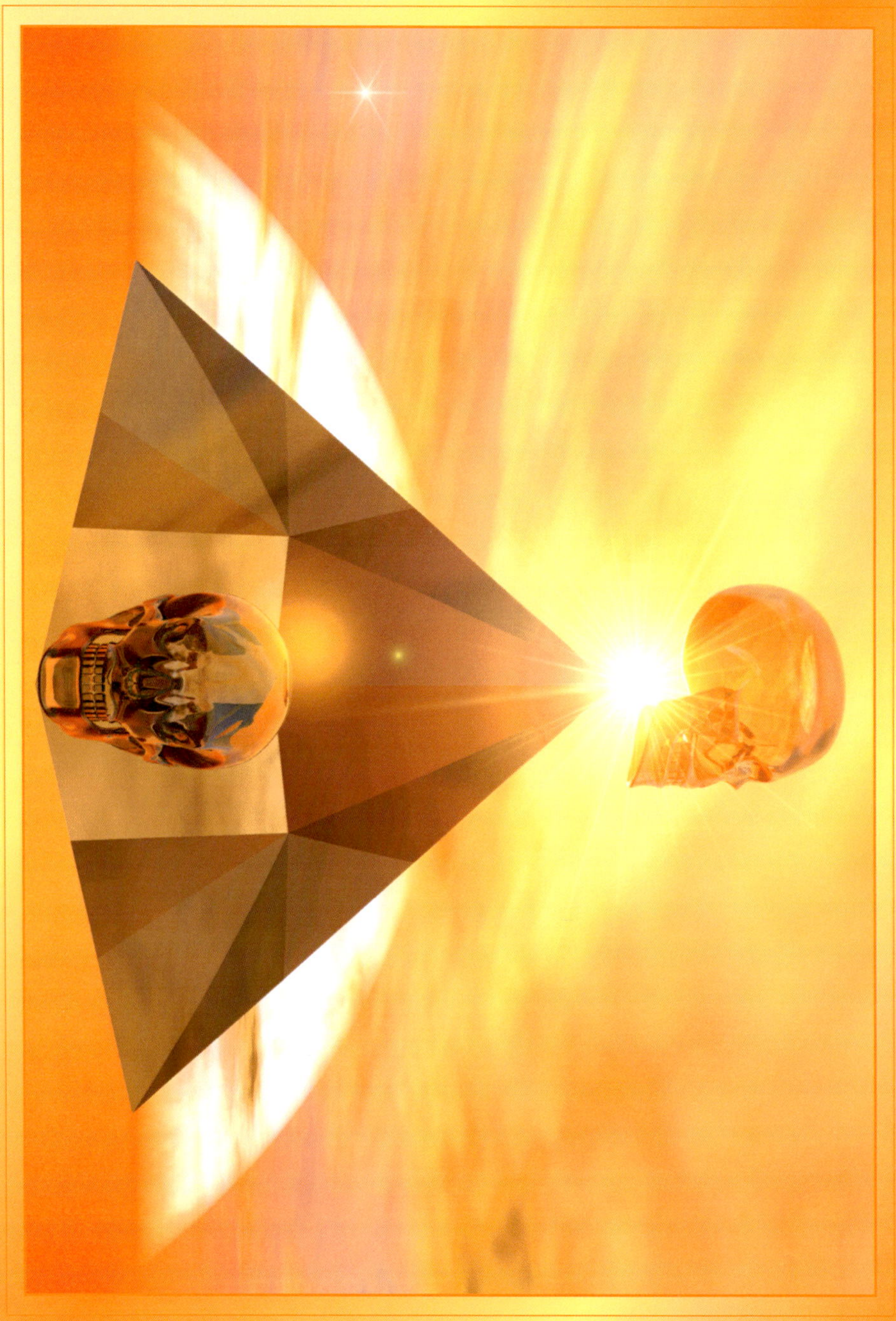

# 28
## ∽ Sacred Space ∾

*"Work with us to energise the base and sacral to invoke joy, passion, creativity, spiritual groundedness and a sense of safety"*

What past emotional issues relating to sexuality, intimacy or security am I releasing?

Who, what or where is sacred to me?

What creative ideas do I need to act on?

### Affirmations

"I am safe and smiling. I see things coming to a positive conclusion very soon."

"I clear any doubts about my abilities and allow my light to shine."

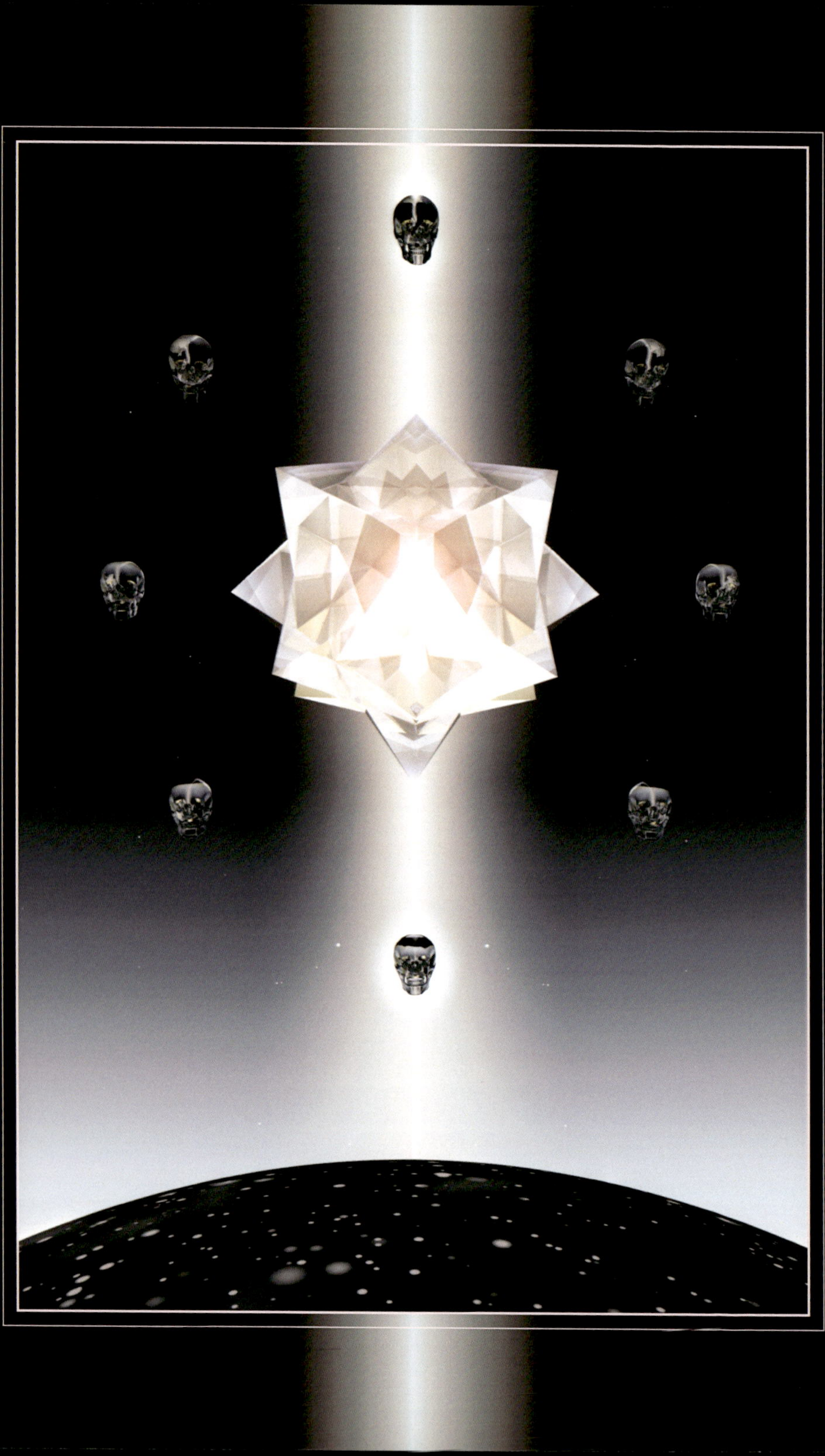

# 29
## ⁓ Star ⁓

*"Work with us for strength, clarity and security in times of major energy shifts"*

How do I stay as energetically clear as possible?

Why is now the right time to accelerate my progress?

What upcoming challenges am I excited about and why?

## Affirmations

"I always see the light in myself and allow it to shine like the brightest star touching Mother Earth and all her inhabitants."

"I embrace the influx of light as it washes through me. I experience it all with ease & grace."

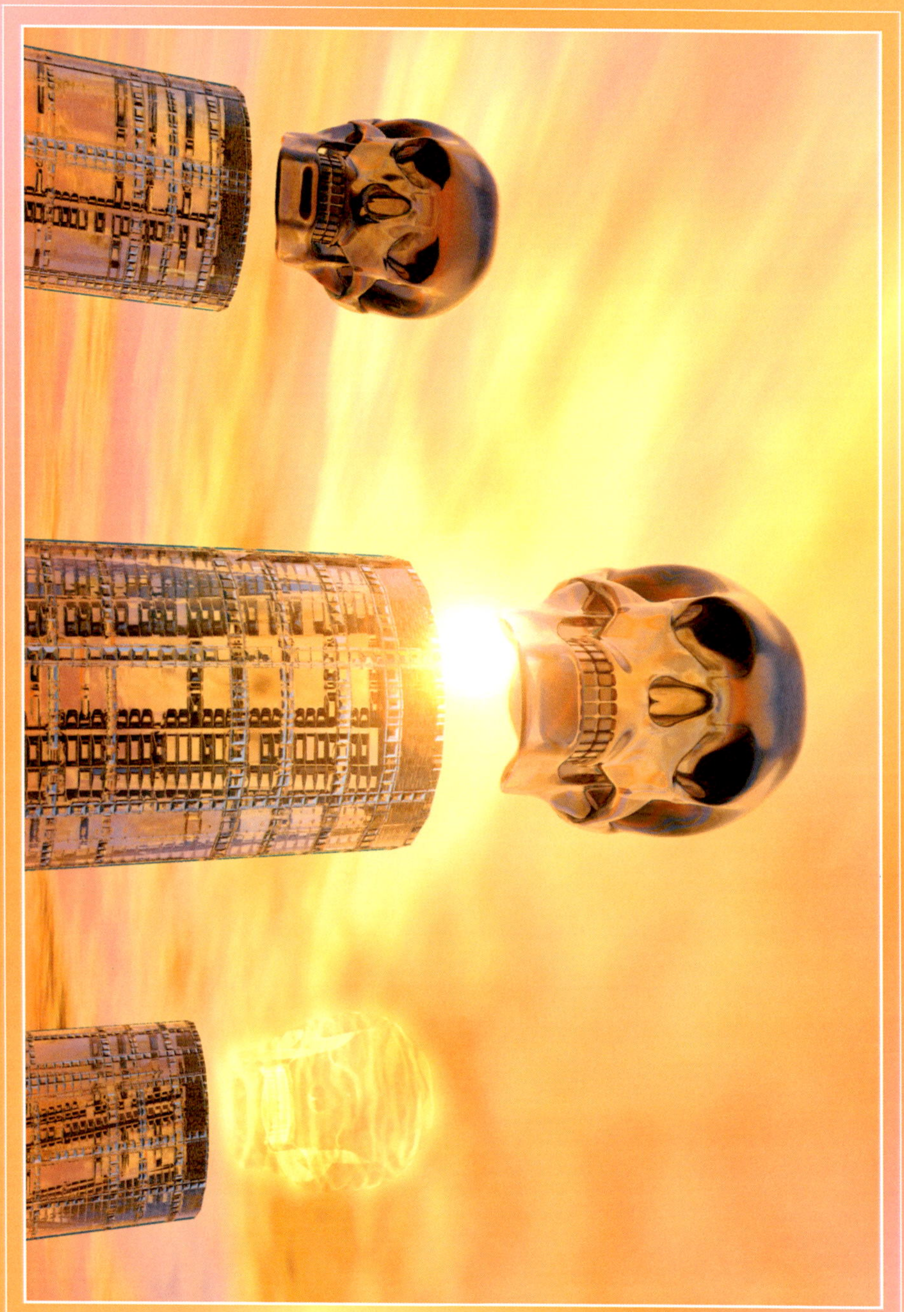

# 30
## ৺ Teleportation ৶

*"Work with us to help you go with the flow and bring a sense of calm & rationality to your emotions"*

How can I relax and allow change to occur?

What new opportunities could emerge if I just slow down?

What is the best way for me to access other dimensions and spiritual help?

---

### Affirmations

"I know my 'off-world' friends are only a thought away and their appearance & assistance can be instant."

"I meditate deeply; so I know I can always find whatever I need, whenever I need it."

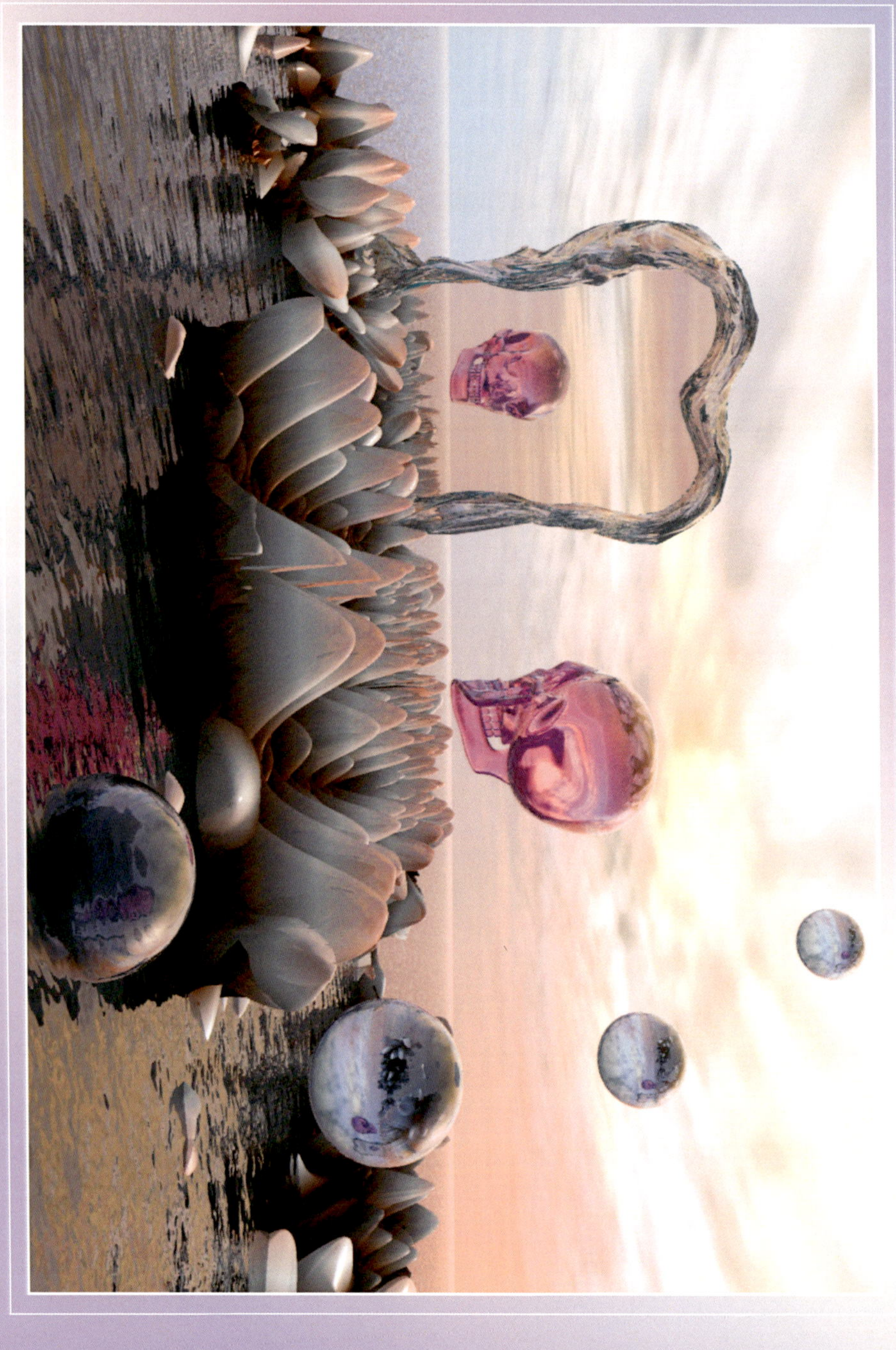

# 31
## ☙ The Mirror ❧

*"Work with us at the heart & crown and within the emotional body to help instil a sense of trust, harmony & compassion"*

What can I learn from other people's reactions to me? How might they be reflecting back something in me?

How can I see the beauty in all things and all people?

What are the qualities I appreciate most about myself?

---

### Affirmations

"As I sit in silent awareness and compassion, I honour that other people's reactions are simply due to their own perceptions."

"I look in the mirror and appreciate all the good qualities within myself."

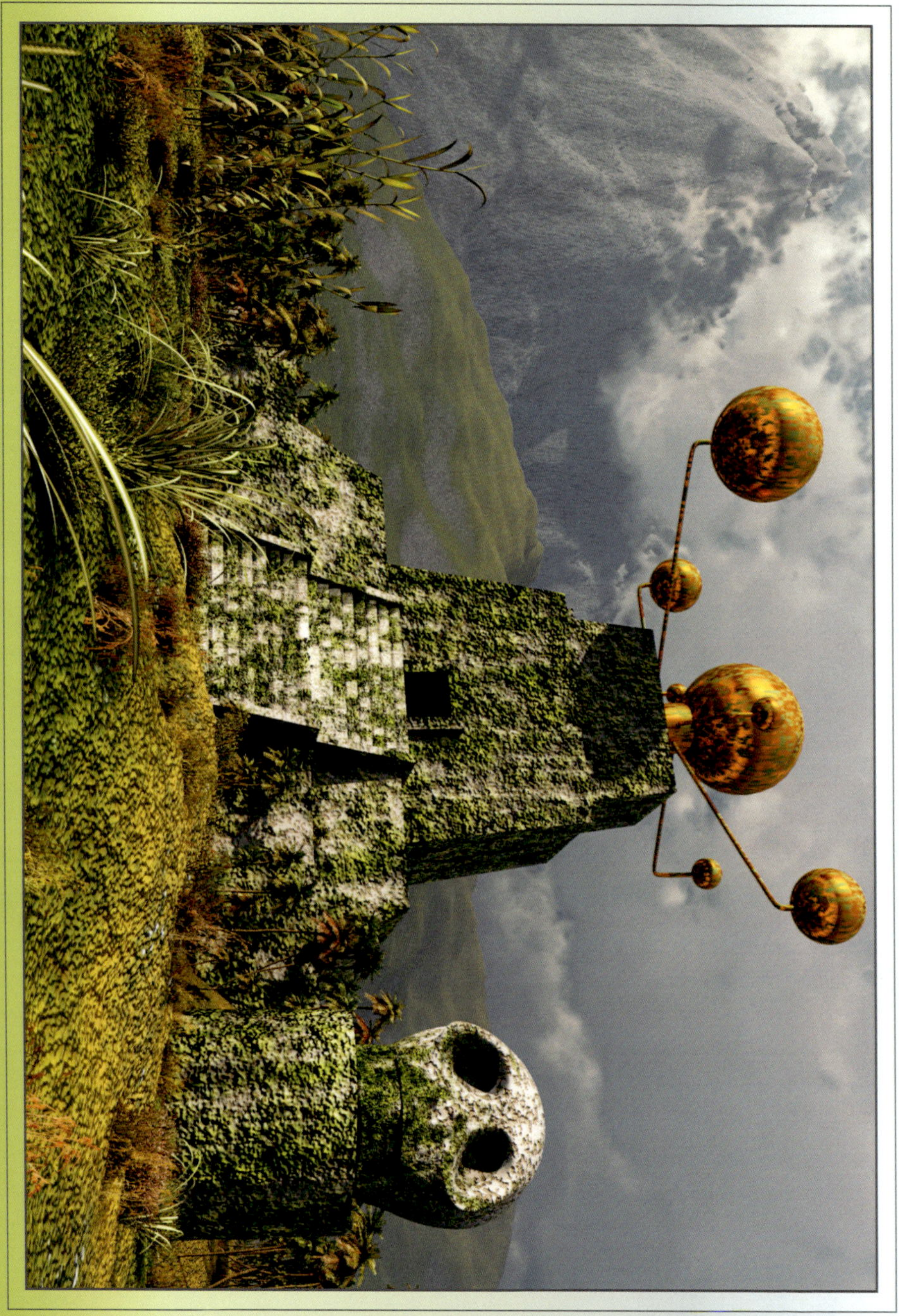

# 32
## ೇ The Observatory ೋ

*"Work with me to feel safe & invisible through apparent conflict, whilst experiencing harmony & acceptance"*

How can two seemingly unrelated things be connected?

How can I mix the old and new to help me achieve my goals?

What do I see when I step aside and take the witness position?

### Affirmations

"I look inwards and in doing so I find my starting point and my destination."

"I accept through compassion and understanding that two seemingly different worlds are really 'part' of the Oneness."

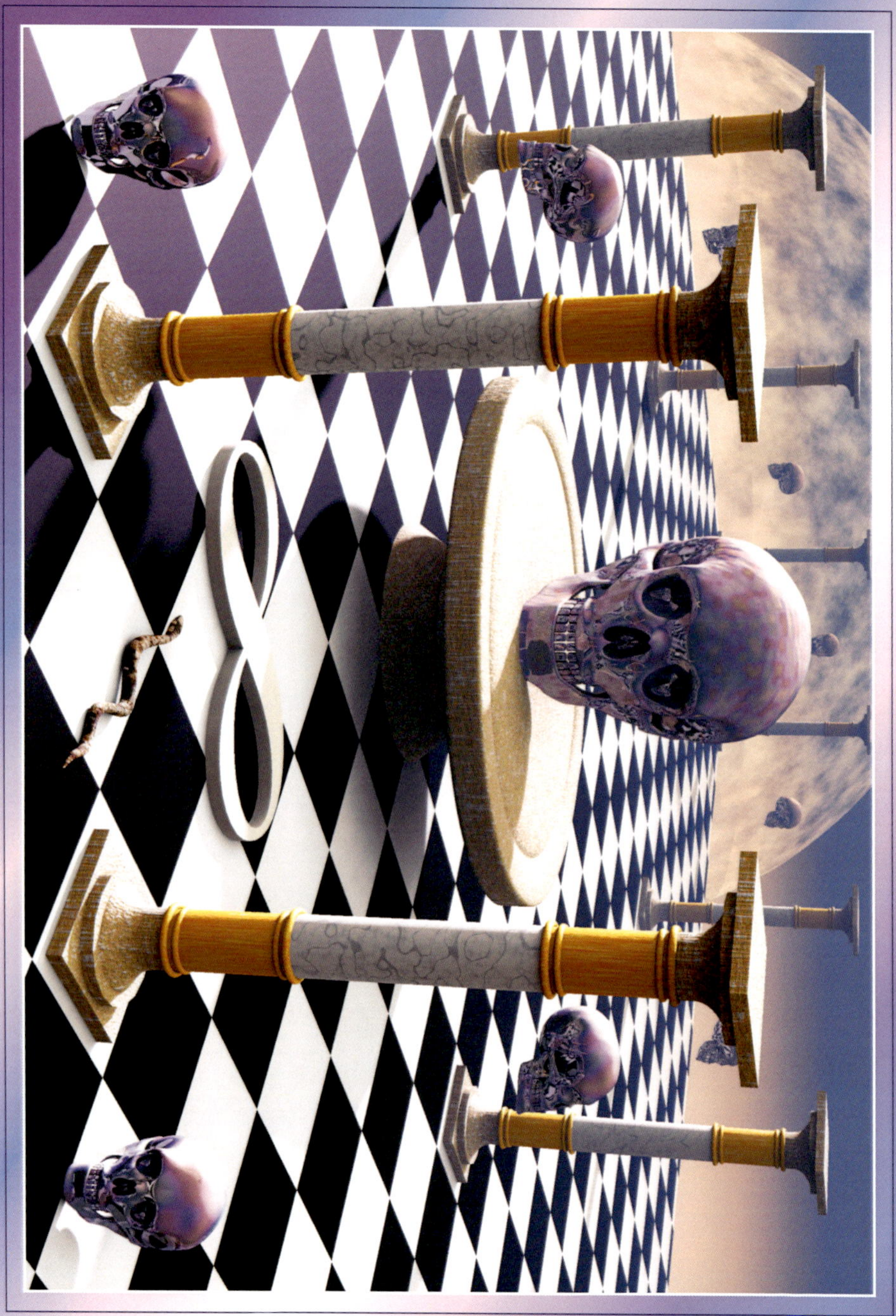

# 33
## ~ The Temple ~

*"Work with us to bring harmony between heart & mind and a balance of the intuitive centres of the third eye & solar plexus"*

How do light and dark go together?

How can I enjoy the process of spiritual transformation?

How am I unifying the power of the heart and the mind?

### Affirmations

"I now stand in my power and work in harmony with others. As I support myself, I support those around me."

"I know in my heart what is right; I take control and make a choice. Now I am ready to move forward."

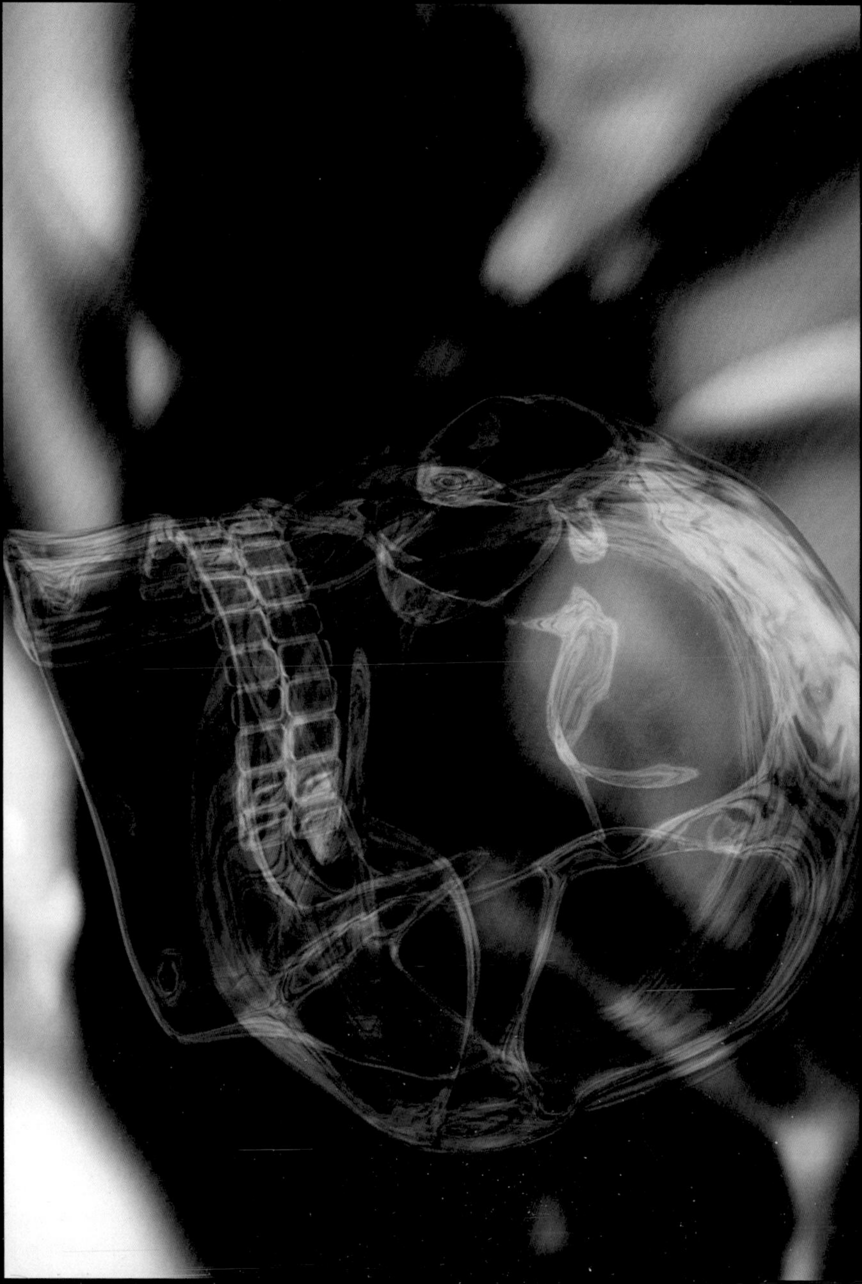

# 34
## ∽ The Void ∾

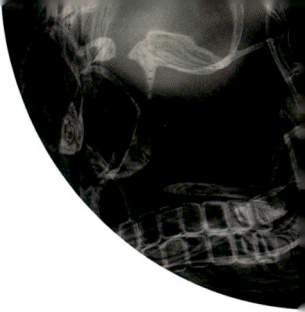

*"Work with me to find strength & power and an overall sense of wellbeing. Know that no one is ever alone"*

How can I embrace the chaos, so a new order can emerge? And why is the void a great place to be?

What new image do I hold of myself?

In what ways am I supported in my life right now? And how do I know?

---

### Affirmations

"I watch this transition with curiosity & fascination as I realise I am eternal and unchanging."

"I allow myself to see the light in all situations."

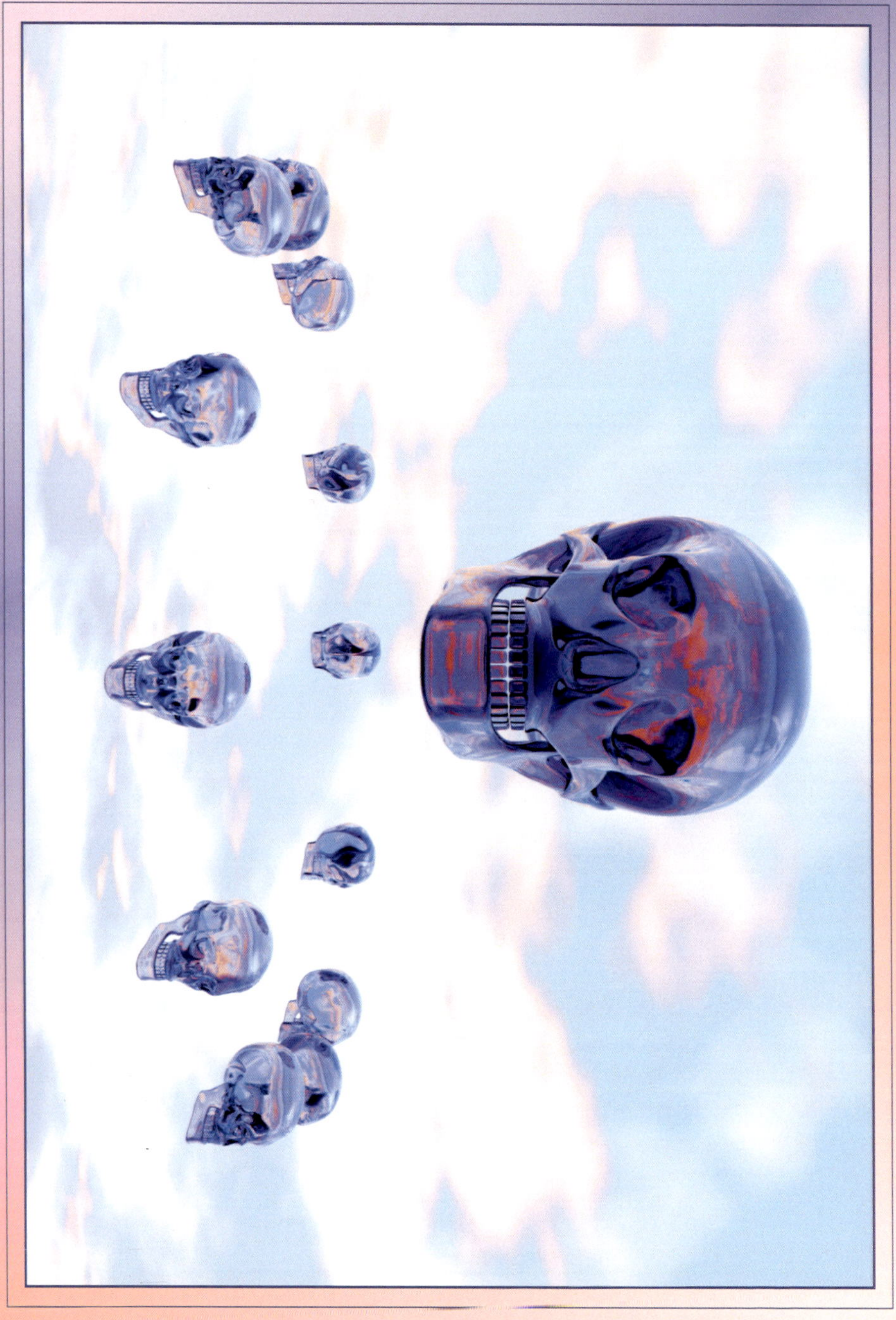

# 35
## ~ Thirteen Skulls ~

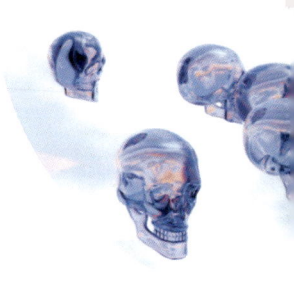

*"Work with us in the outer bodies, especially in times of spiritual and emotional shift to instil a sense of trust and tranquillity"*

In what ways can I experience unity, unconditional love, peace and acceptance right now?

What is the nature of my true self?

Who is the new member of my family? And what will they teach me?

### Affirmations

"I accept with ease & grace the current transformation going on within and around me."

"I allow the ancient wisdom stored within me to flow forth for the benefit of all."

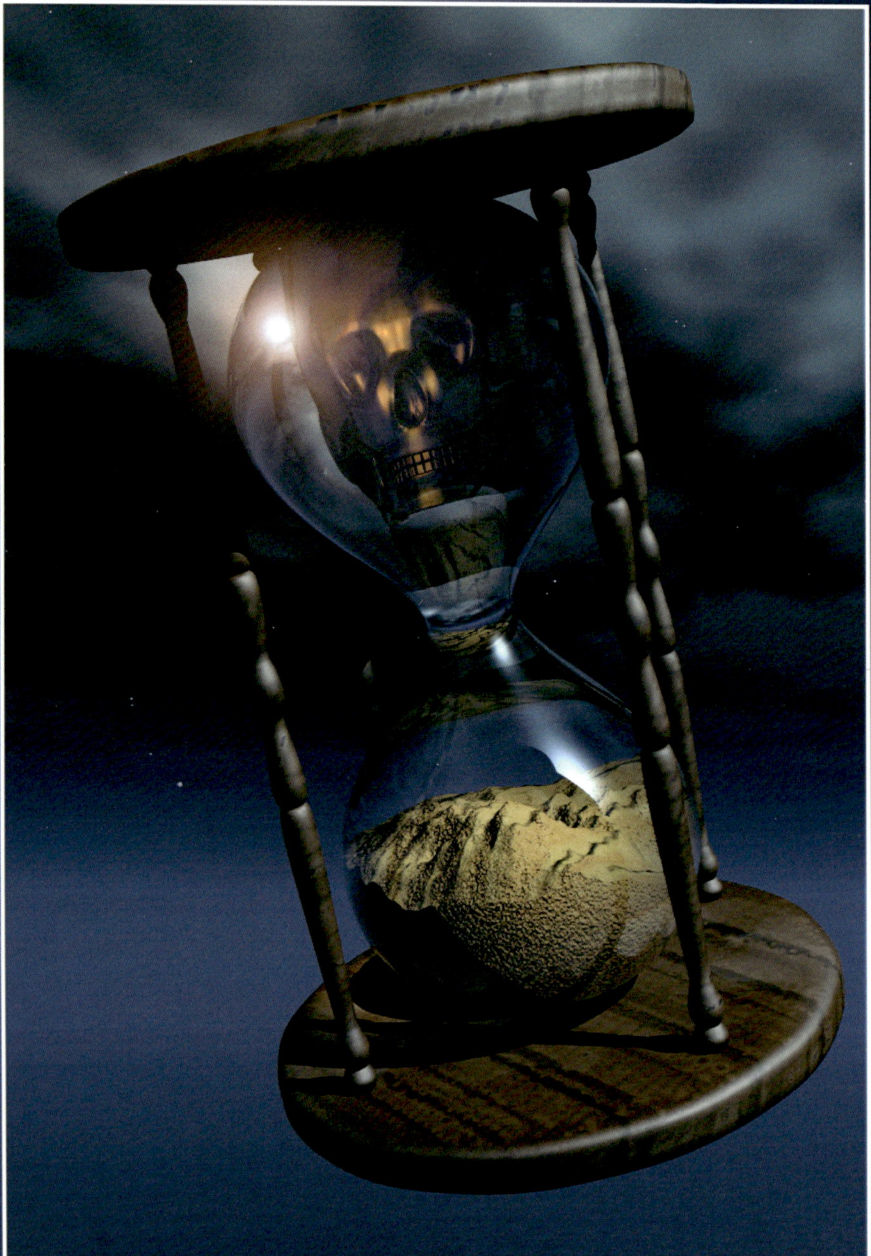

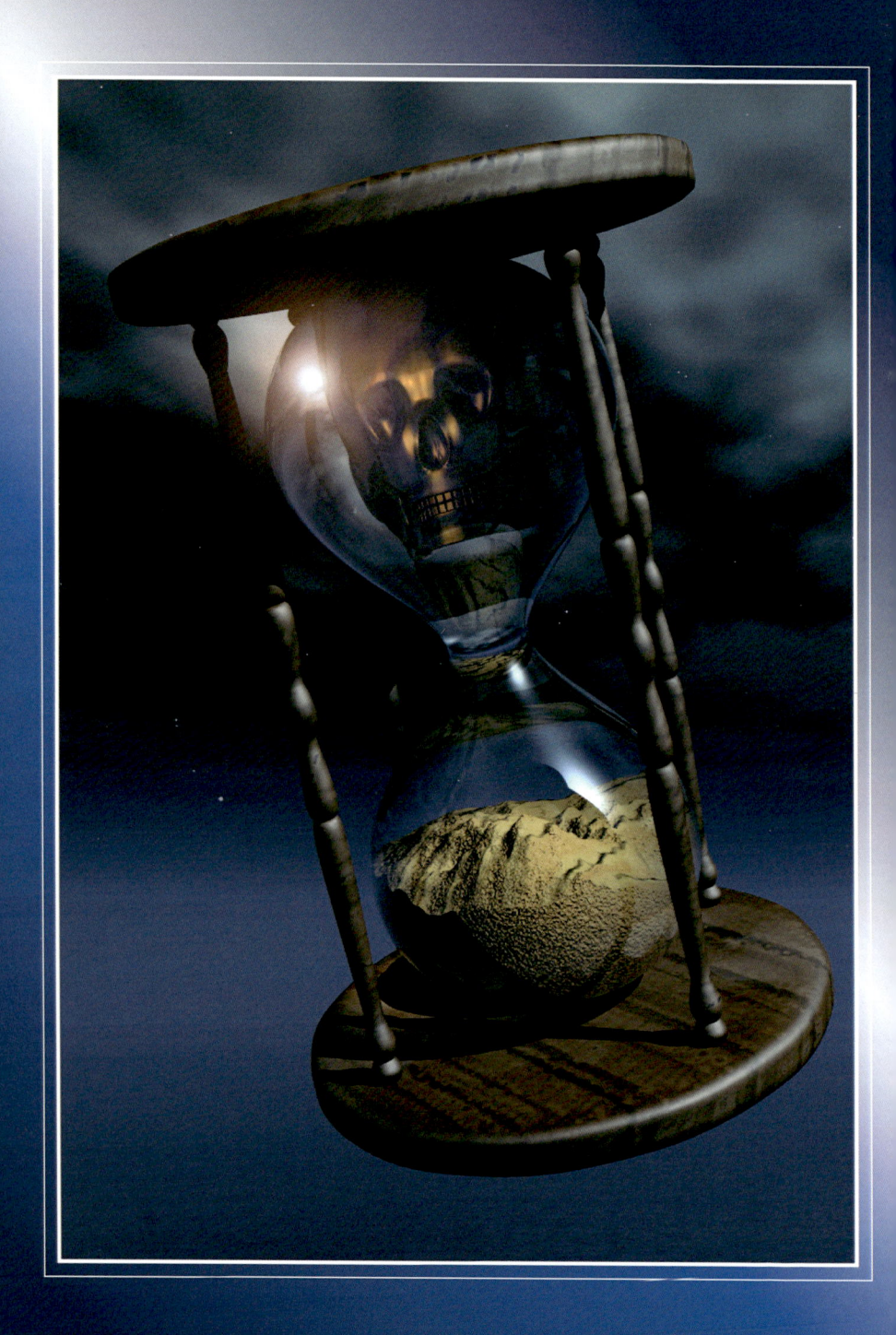

# 36
## ~ Time ~

*"Work with me to energise the throat, third eye & base. I can also assist in saying 'no' to people, so that time is not wasted"*

How am I experiencing the flow of time?

Who are my Timekeepers today?

How can I take greater control of my time to help me achieve my goals?

### Affirmations

"I know that everything happens in divine time and with absolute precision."

"I command more time. Thank You! It is done, it is done, it is done."

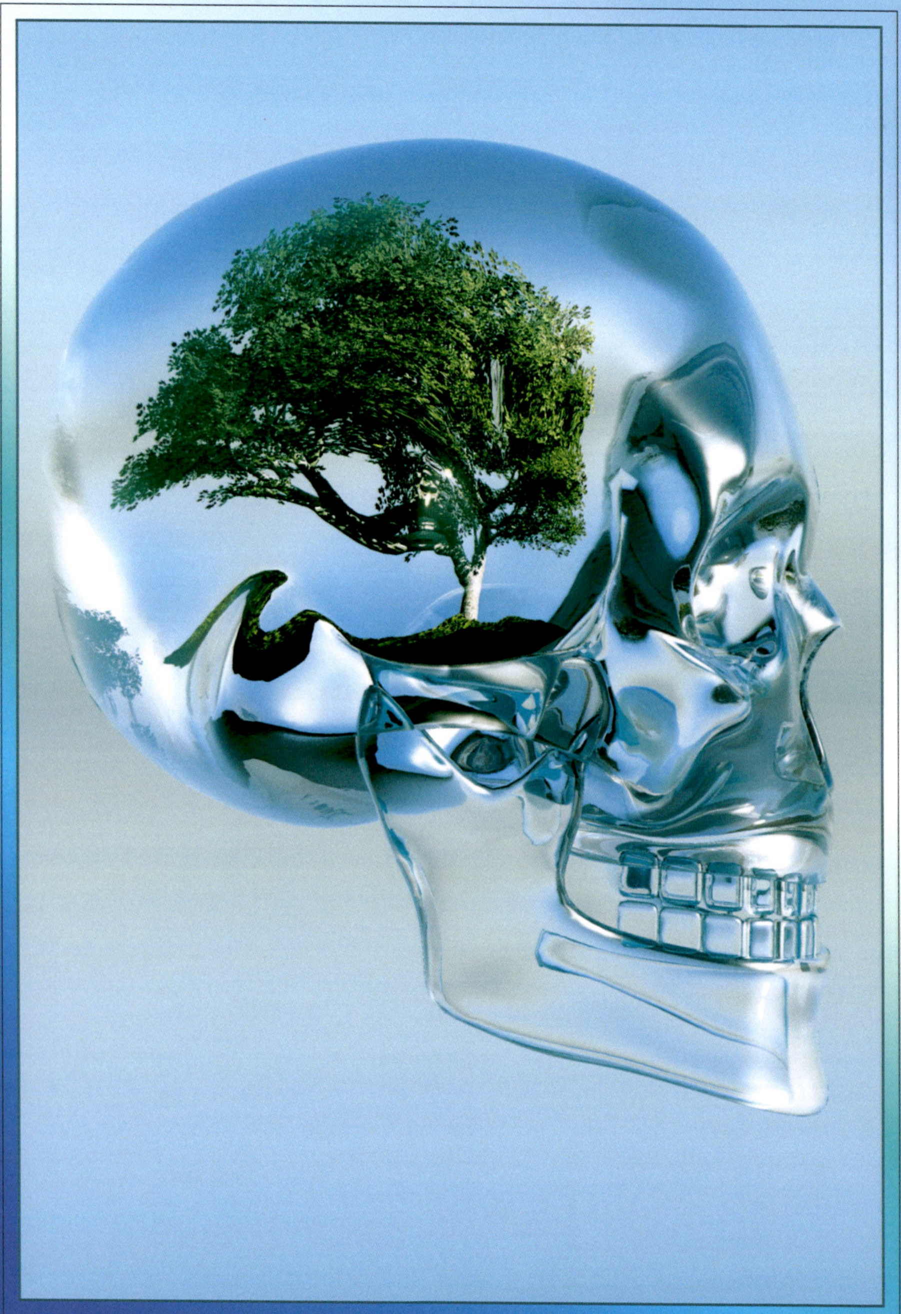

## 37
### ꙮ Tree of Knowledge ꙮ

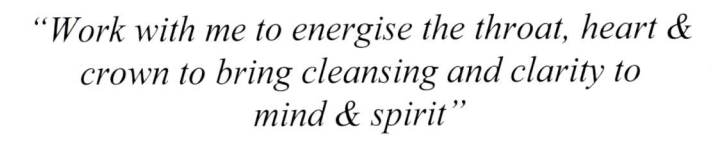

*"Work with me to energise the throat, heart & crown to bring cleansing and clarity to mind & spirit"*

What knowledge and skills do I need now? Where can I find them?

How do I make learning simple and fun?

Where is my heart guiding me and why is this perfect for me right now?

### Affirmations

*"I trust in the universe - the right books, teachers and pathway are coming to me now."*

*"I am accessing ancient wisdom and practical skills to bring my dreams into reality."*

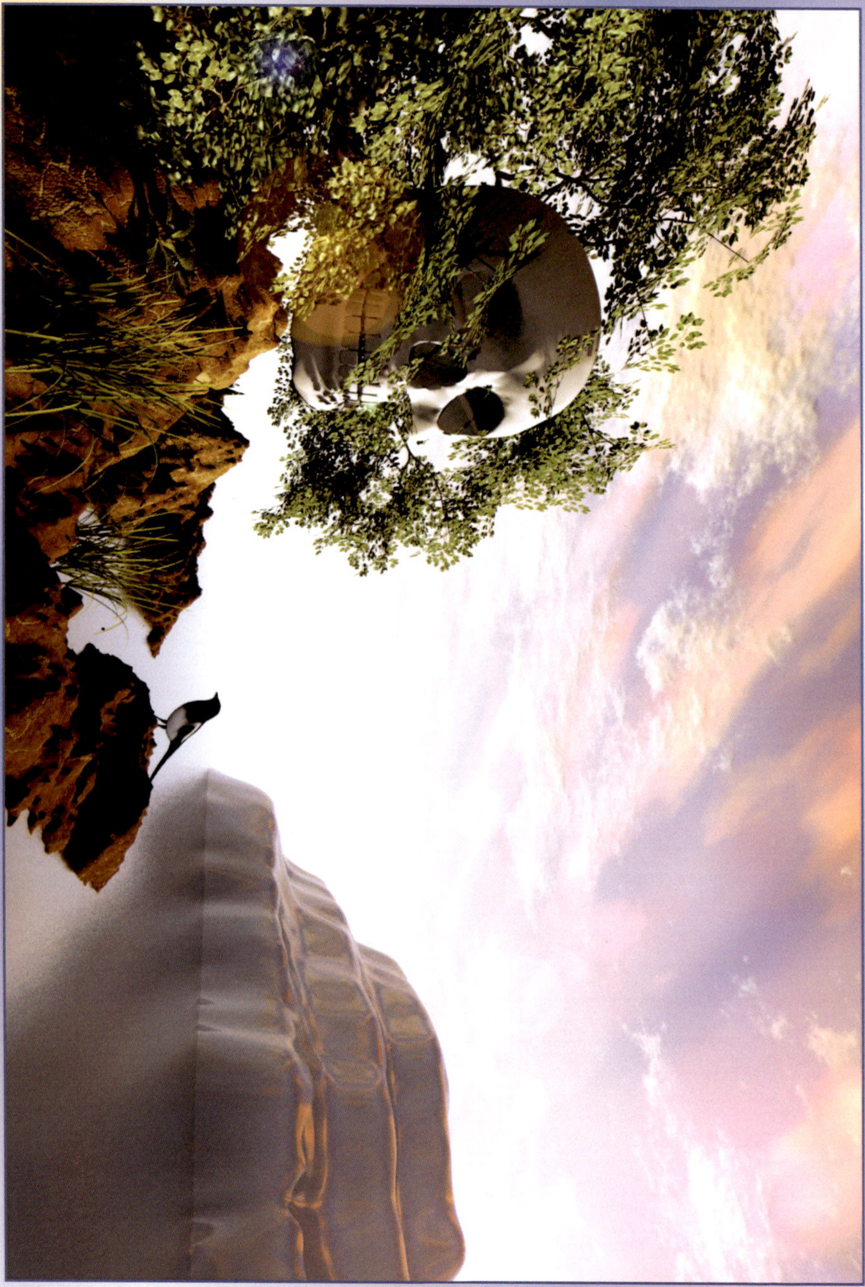

# 38
## ❦ Trusted Friend ❧

*"Work with me to feel emotionally stable and to easily share what's in your heart"*

What is in my heart that I need to share?

How can I create perfect harmony between logic and intuition?

What benefits will I gain from taking the next step forward?

## Affirmations

"I love myself and trust that all change is good."

"I understand appropriate use of spiritual knowledge and share my love, light & healing power."

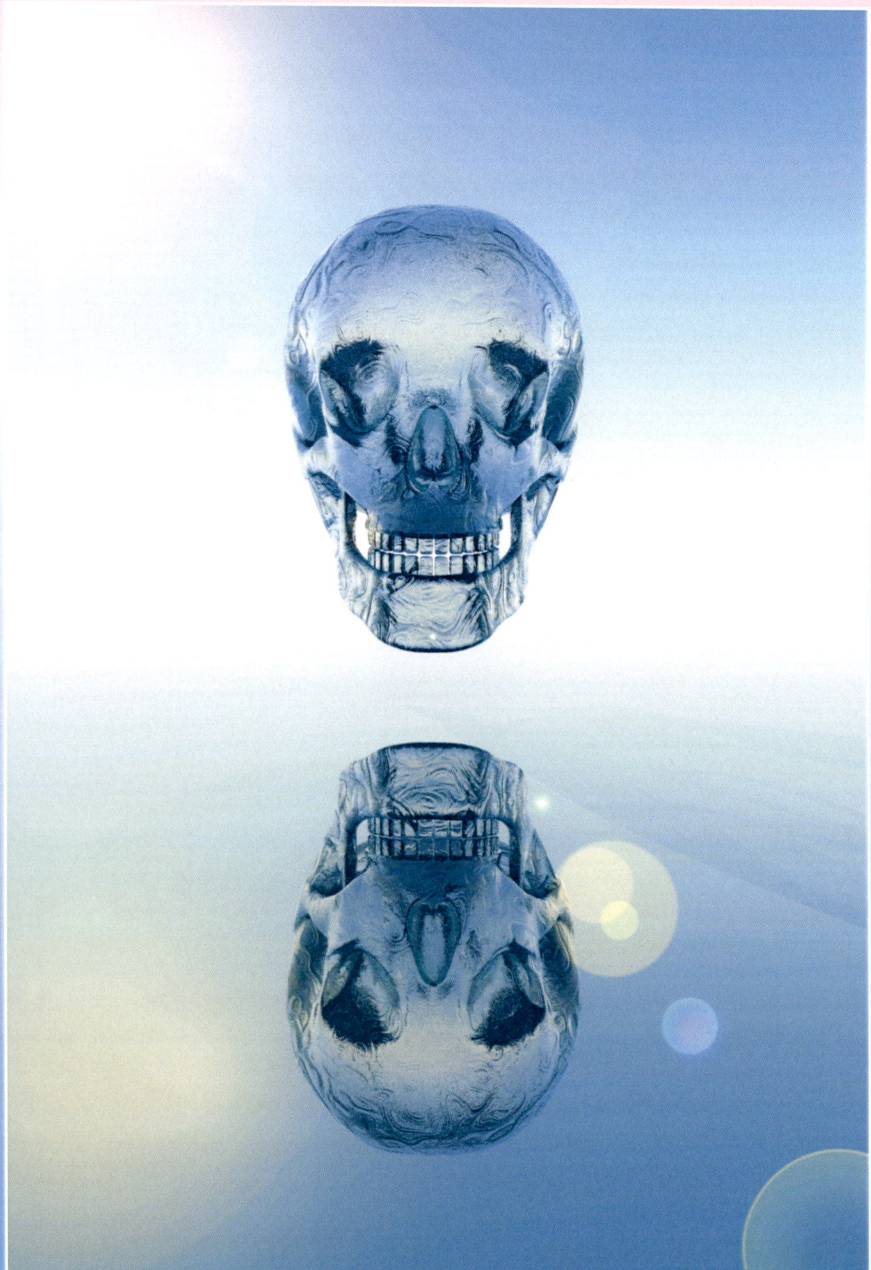

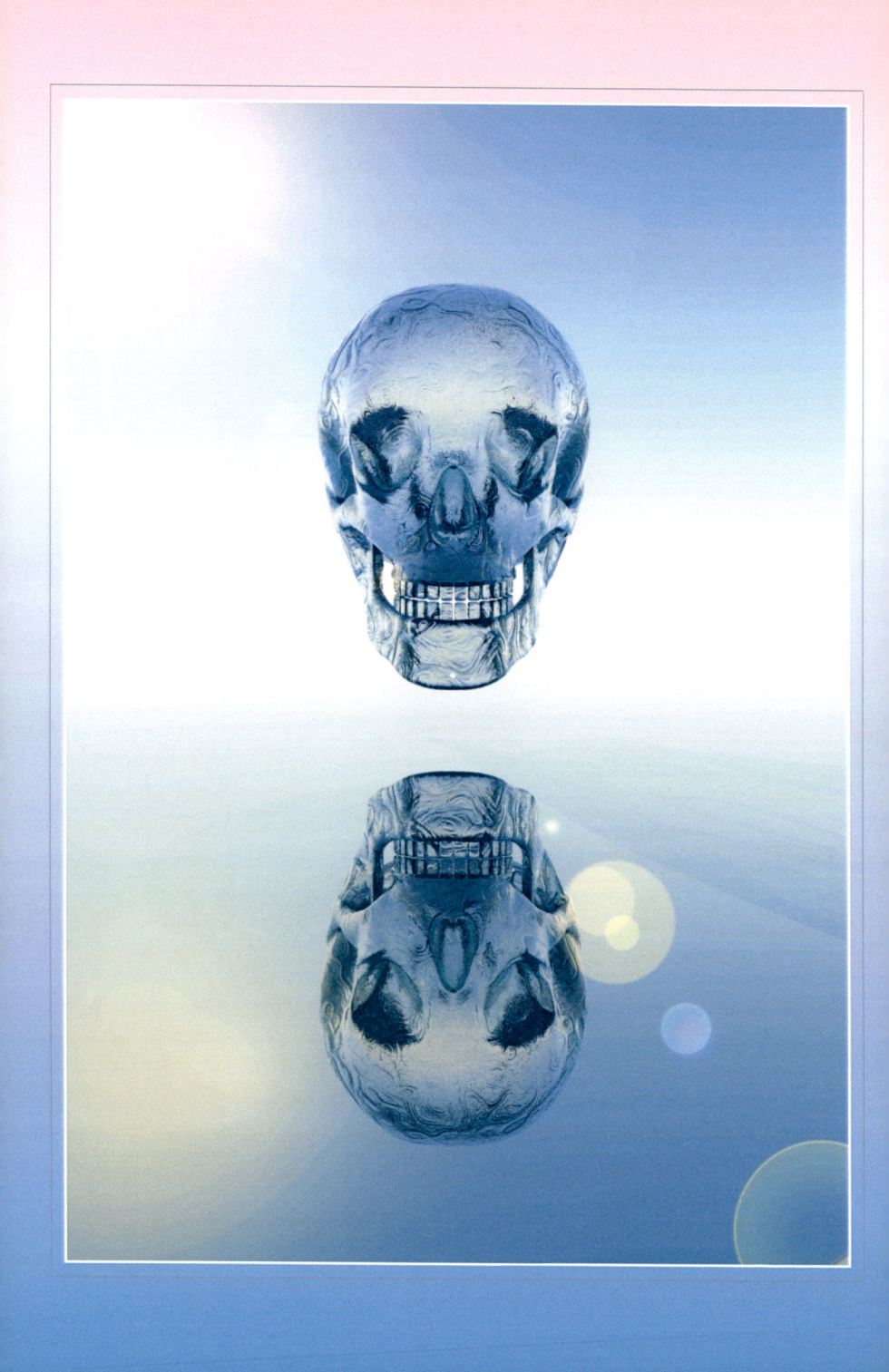

# 39
## ⁓ Two Worlds ⁓

*"Work with us to activate the soul star, crown, throat & heart and to connect to the Divine for higher & deeper communication"*

How do I safely walk between two worlds?

If ever I encounter lost souls, how best do I help them?

How does my concept of myself limit me? And how will I change that?

## Affirmations

"I trust in my connection to Source and raise my vibration as I walk & work in many worlds."

"I honour within me the healer, medium, lightworker, shaman, counsellor, sound bringer and everything I Am."

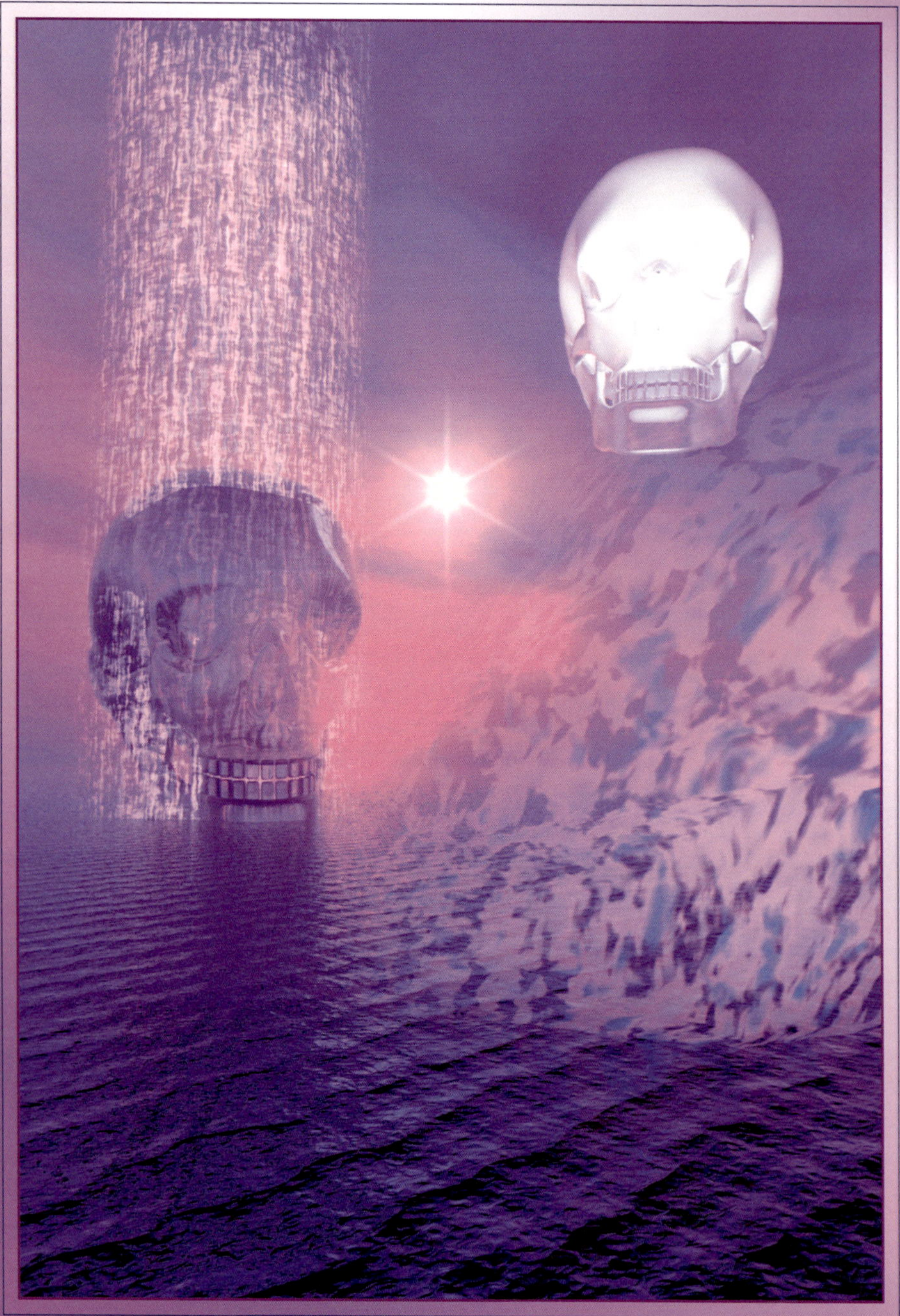

# 40
## ⁓ Violet Flame ⁓

*"Work with us to clear & balance an overactive solar plexus and to stimulate visions, dreams & clairvoyance"*

Where do I pick up the most debris? And how can I quickly & easily release it?

How can the Violet Flame assist me?

What dreams should I be working with now?

### Affirmations

*"I rise like a phoenix from the ashes and step into my true power."*

*"I access & honour my spiritual teaching work and share my truths, knowledge & wisdom for the good of all."*

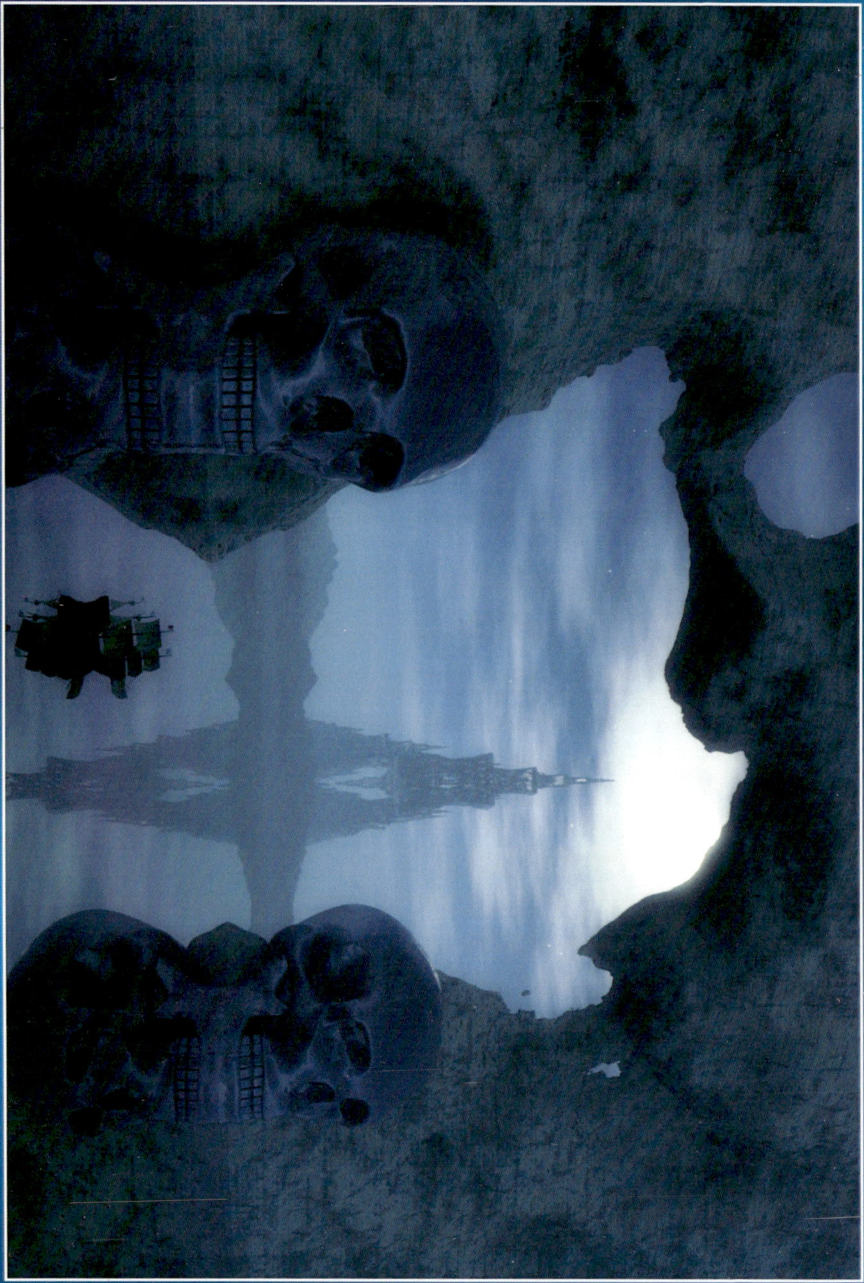

# 41
## Voyage of Discovery

*"Work with us to energise the base, throat & third eye and to help bring emotional & mental strength"*

How will transmuting past negative vibrations benefit me?

What great things am I not seeing, doing or experiencing that are right under my nose?

How can moving into the unknown expand my possibilities?

### Affirmations

"I know the 'dark' will retreat in the presence of my light, so I find courage and I take the plunge."

"I follow my heart & spirit into the unknown and embark on a new & exciting journey."

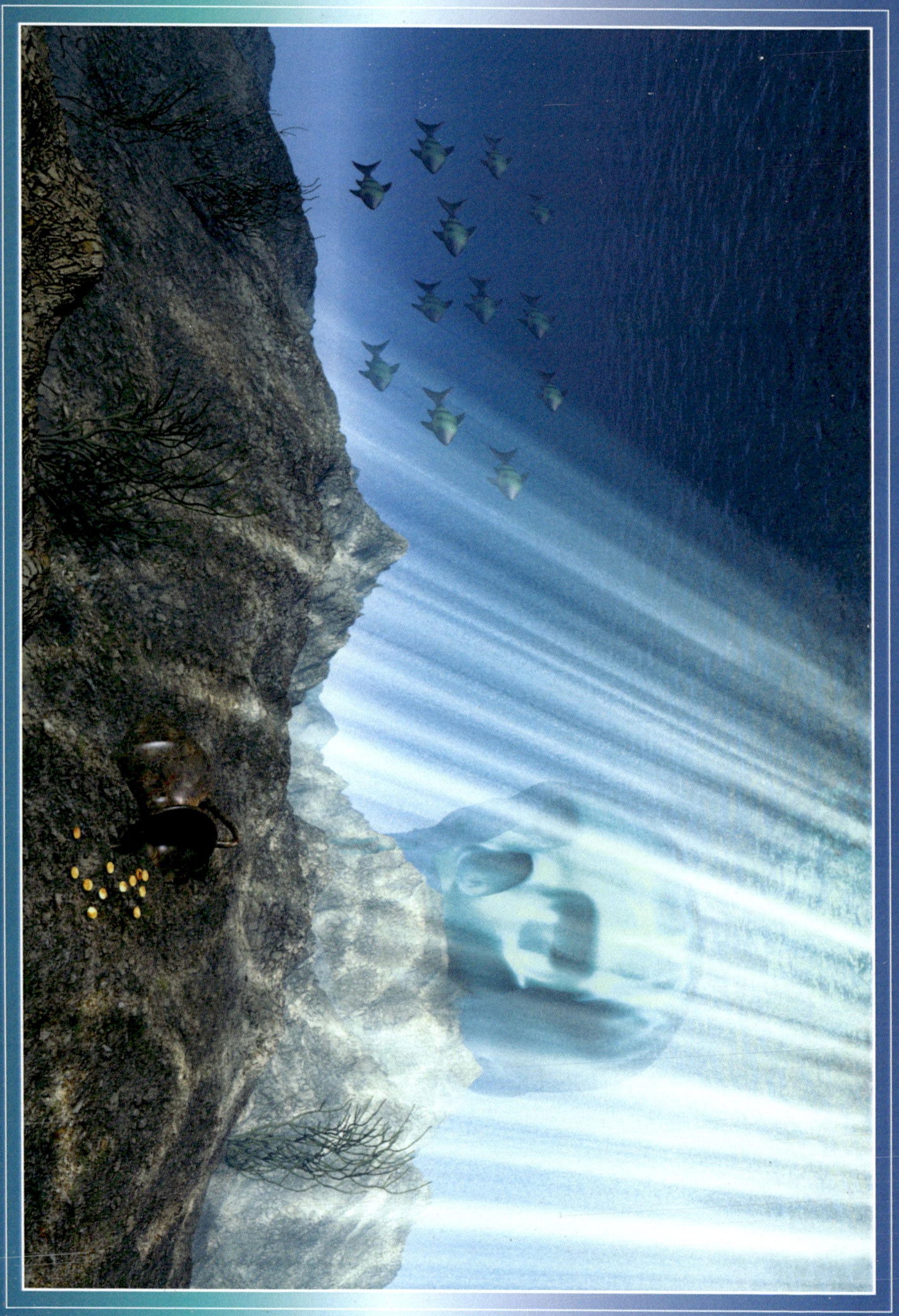

# 42
## ∽ Water ∾

*"Work with me to energise the throat chakra and stimulate forthright communication. I can also help stabilize unsettled emotions"*

What deep seated thoughts and feelings will I allow to wash away?

How can I create a deeper communication with my inner self?

In what ways can I access greater creativity and abundance?

### Affirmations

"I release that which no longer serves me and allow the healing light of the Crystal Skull Collective to shine through me."

"I access the communicator and activate the networker within me."

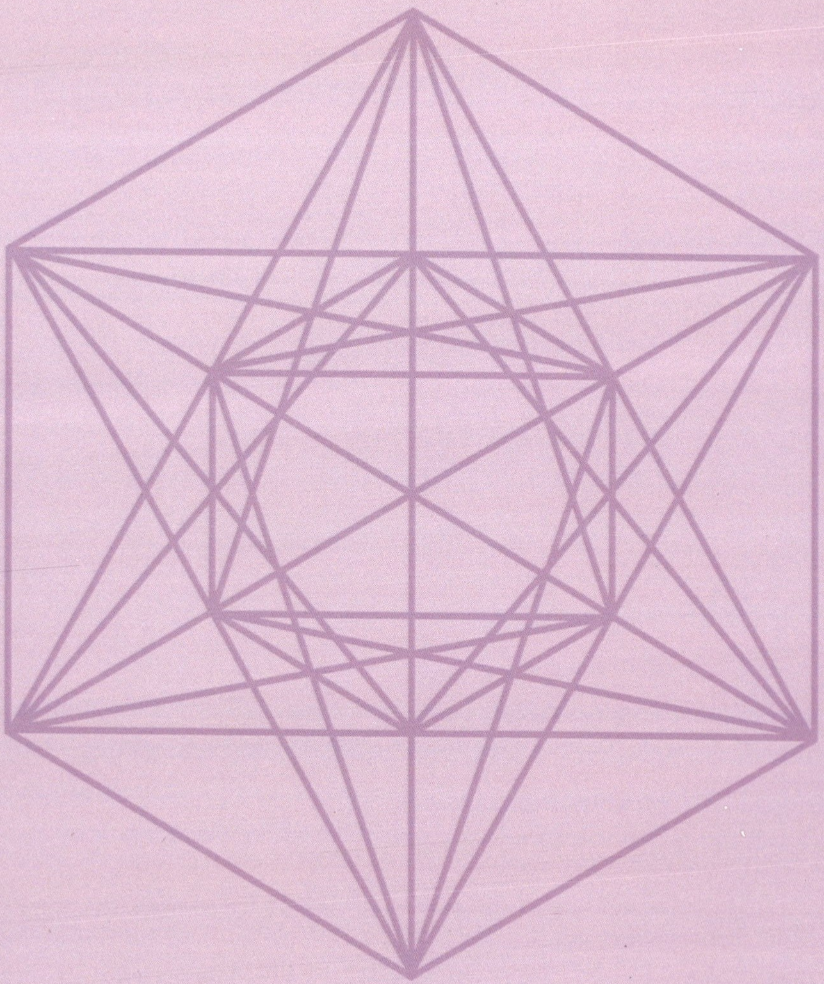